Hon. Howell Cobb.

Howell Cobb

FROM A PHOTOGRAPH TAKEN WHILE

SECRETARY OF THE UNITED STATES TREASURY.

A MEMORIAL VOLUME

OF THE

HON. HOWELL COBB

OF GEORGIA.

EDITED BY

SAMUEL BOYKIN.

" He was a man, take him for all in all,
I shall not look upon his like again.

PHILADELPHIA
J. B. LIPPINCOTT & CO.
1870.

LIPPINCOTT'S PRESS
PHILADELPHIA.

CONTENTS.

PREFACE.

THIS book is not designed to be a Biography of the late Gen. COBB. To some future pen, able to do justice to so noble a subject, that task is left. All that is now attempted is a memorial tribute to that distinguished gentleman.

No man has, for many years, died in Georgia leaving behind him more numerous or more appreciating and attached friends than Gov. Cobb. His name was a household word in many of the homes of our State. He was loved by the lowly and honored by the great. In private, in the domestic circle, at the Bar and in the loftiest walks of political life he was regarded as an amiable, able, patriotic and benevolent man. His sudden death in the prime of life, and when his fame had already pervaded the American Union, called forth numerous and eulogistic testimonials to his admirable character. They exalt him almost to the acme of human excellence. And, as if to crown his career and character with the most resplendent glory, it was vouchsafed to him to die a Christian.

Tributes to his memory were promptly rendered by the Bar and the People. These and the discourses delivered at the funeral, which were reported expressly for this work, the editor has collected and presents in this volume. They will be found exceedingly interesting, and worthy of permanent record. In addition, the editor has been kindly permitted to publish a few brief sketches of Gov. Cobb's life and character—the free and voluntary contributions of distinguished friends and contemporaries. He has ventured to contribute little from his own pen besides such statements as seemed to him to be appropriate as connecting links in the series.

The volume is graced with two steel engravings—one representing Gov. Cobb when Secretary of the United States Treasury, and the other representing his appearance at the time of his death. Both are capital likenesses, and add greatly to the value of the book.

The editor is satisfied that the whole will be read with interest, and that this unpretending effort to honor a great and good man will be acceptable to the public.

S. B.

Macon, Georgia, May 1, 1869.

BIOGRAPHICAL SKETCH.

BIOGRAPHICAL SKETCH

OF

GENERAL HOWELL COBB,

OF GEORGIA.

IT would be a narrow as well as erroneous view of what pertains to the welfare of society to confine inquiry to the mere external and professional life of those whose fortune it has been to bear a prominent part in the control of the great interests of nations. While their history derives a great part of its interest from the public events with which they have been connected, their character, their morals, their intellectual faculties and their use of the gifts with which the Creator has endowed them present a still more interesting field of historical investigation, since it is true of all nations, especially of republics, that in proportion as the individuals who conduct the affairs of government are wise, virtuous and capable, or unwise, vicious and incompetent, the republic advances and prospers or retrogrades and decays in all that constitutes its greatness and its glory.

Of the statesmen of the United States, few have occupied a more prominent position or a greater and more continuous hold upon the public confidence than HOWELL COBB. He bore a leading part in some of the greatest scenes of the republic's history. He has filled important positions of trust and honor in the councils of the United States and of the State of Georgia. From an age when most men are deemed too young and inexperienced to participate prominently in public affairs he was clothed with the highest and most responsible duties by his countrymen; and when he rendered back his life to the God who gave it, the voice of lamentation and mourning which went up from every part of Georgia proclaimed the esteem in which his lifelong service was held by those who had confided in him, who knew him best and who were best fitted to judge his character.

It would not be consistent with the purpose of this work to do more than draw an outline sketch of the political life of General Cobb. In a volume which is principally composed of the tributes which were paid to his memory immediately after his decease by public bodies with which he had been prominently connected for many years, and by friends with whom he was intimately associated in public and in private life, it would be inappropriate to dwell at any length upon the political questions in the discussion of which he bore a leading part, or by giving occasion to criticism or difference of political opinion to mix the thorns of partisan and sectional discord among the flowers of love, reverence and admiration which the hand of friendship designs to weave into a wreath to be deposited affectionately upon his tomb.

Howell Cobb was born in Jefferson county, Georgia, on the 7th of September, 1816. His father, Colonel John A. Cobb, was a native of North Carolina, in which state his ancestors settled long prior to the Revolution, and whence Colonel Cobb, while quite young, moved to Georgia and became a planter and owner of large landed possessions.

General Cobb's mother, Sarah R. Cobb, was the daughter of Thomas Reede Rootes, Esq., of Fredericksburg, Va.—one of the most famous jurists of his day in the Old Dominion.

Besides the subject of this sketch, Colonel and Mrs. Cobb had two sons and four daughters—namely, General Thomas Reede Rootes Cobb, the eminent lawyer, statesman and soldier, who fell at the battle of Fredericksburg, December 12, 1862; Major John B. Cobb, who is still living; Laura, wife of Williams Rutherford, Professor of Mathematics in the University of Georgia; Mildred, wife of Col. Luther J. Glenn; Mary, wife of Doctor J. M. Johnson; and Martha, wife of Major J. C. Whitner.

The Cobbs are of Welsh extraction. Their descent has been traced back to a distinguished family of the name in the days of Llewellyn, and among the Cobbs now living in Wales the Christian name Howell is frequently found to exist.

Colonel Cobb, though a man of very great ability and universally beloved and respected, never took any part in public affairs. The care of a large family and the management of an extensive and complicated property absorbed all his attention.

While Howell Cobb was still quite a child his parents moved from Jefferson county to Athens, Clarke county, where the schools and the University afforded better means of educating their children than could be found in the country.

After the usual course of preparatory education at the grammar school of Mr. Fulton, Howell Cobb entered the University, where he graduated with honor in 1834. His childhood and boyhood, though unmarked by any event calling for particular notice, displayed those qualities of the head and of the heart for which in manhood he was distinguished among men.

The wonderful rapidity with which his intellect grasped any subject which engaged his attention, his unselfish nature, his generosity of disposition, his love of truth and his hatred of meanness and falsehood, were the prominent characteristics of his boyhood as they were of his maturer years. Full of life, of exuberant animal spirits, fond of fun and manly sport, he often neglected his studies, and not unfrequently transgressed the strict rules of scholastic and collegiate discipline; but the ready candor with which he acknowledged his fault, the generous anxiety with which he strove to relieve his companions from blame and punishment, the utter absence of mean motives or unmanly acts, even where his breach of regulation or disobedience of orders was most flagrant, and his unswerving fidelity to truth at all times and upon all occasions, always atoned for his misdeeds, and, where they did not cause an entire remission of punishment, invariably mitigated its severity.

His genial manners, ready wit, intellectual quickness and high principles caused him to be universally beloved by his companions and won for him the affectionate regard of all his tutors and instructors, of whom those who are still living were among the most attached of his friends, and are now among those who are most deeply afflicted by his death.

Love of his parents and love of truth were the most marked characteristics of his youth; and to them may be traced that remarkable self-control, that tender regard for the feelings of others, that candor, uprightness of purpose, fidelity to duty, charity, forbearance toward everything but meanness and falsehood, which marked his career from its commencement to its close.

In the month of August, 1834, he graduated, taking the third honor in his class, and soon after commenced the study of the law in the office of General Harden, then one of the most successful legal practitioners in Northern Georgia. In 1836 he was admitted to the bar, and gave such evidence of character, ability and legal attainment that in the following year he was elected by the Legislature Solicitor-General of the Western Circuit, by which he became the legal representative of the State in all cases civil and criminal in which the State is a party. He held the office for the full term of three years for which he was elected, and discharged its onerous and difficult duties with a skill, vigor and fidelity which had never been surpassed upon the circuit. With surprising rapidity he took rank at the bar among the first and most gifted of its members, acquired a lucrative practice, and by his frank cordiality of manner, kindliness of heart and faithful attention to the interests of his clients, won the confidence and esteem of all—bench, lawyers and suitors—with whom he came in contact.

A few months after he left the University, and before his admission to the bar, he married Miss Mary Ann Lamar, daughter of Colonel Zachariah Lamar, of Baldwin county—one of the wealthiest, most influential and most estimable citizens in Georgia.

The Lamars are of French origin, and were

among the Huguenot families who took refuge in America after the Revocation of the Edict of Nantes, and who in proportion to their numbers have contributed more largely to the intellectual progress, refinement and material advancement of the country than any other class of the population of the United States.

General Cobb's marriage was the most fortunate event of his life, and produced the best influences on his subsequent career. Devotedly attached to his wife and children, never so happy as when at home surrounded by his family and friends, he made his house the centre of his joys, regarding his wife as his best, truest and most capable counselor, and making her wishes, her comfort and her happiness the first object of his life.

To estimate the real happiness of his married life, the perfect confidence and community of tastes and feelings which existed without interruption between him and his wife until the hour of his death—to understand the mutuality of affection between them and their children—it is necessary to have been admitted to intimacy in his family circle; and those who have enjoyed this privilege, and have seen how unselfish love, unlimited confidence and sincere esteem reigned supreme in that household, are at a loss whether most to admire the affectionate husband, fond father and genial companion, the devoted wife, faithful and intelligent helpmate and loving mother, whose precept and example always harmonized because they were always prompted by fervent piety and purity of thought and deed, or the obedient and tenderly attached children, whose love of their parents and of each other seemed to be the mainspring of their action.

During the three years of his service as Solicitor-General, which brought him into close contact with the people of that portion of Northern Georgia comprised in the Western Circuit, he became universally popular with all classes.

After a short time passed in the active practice of his profession, he was called on by the people to represent them in the Federal Legislature.

In October, 1842, shortly after the passage of the act for the apportionment of representatives by districts according to the sixth census, but before the Legislature of Georgia had time to adapt the State law to the new Congressional enactment, Howell Cobb was elected to Congress upon the general ticket, and took his seat in December, 1843, at the commencement of the Twenty-eighth Congress.

Mr. Cobb was a Democrat of the Jackson school. He was sincerely attached to the Union of the States, while at the same time he was uncompromisingly opposed to the surrender of the practical rights of the States as coequal members of the federal family of sovereign commonwealths. He was always ready to make any sacrifice short of honor and principle to preserve and perpetuate the Union as it was framed and designed by its builders; but he would never agree to yield any of the individual rights of the States guaranteed to them by the Constitution, which clearly defines the powers and authority which the States severally and collectively agreed to confer upon the General Government as their common agent, taking especial care specifically to reserve to themselves all other powers which were not thus conferred in express terms. While this was his position, he never dealt in abstractions. He was no hair-splitter in construing the Constitution, nor did he allow theories to obscure his eminently practical view of the political field.

He was opposed to the nullification projects of Mr. Calhoun, and when sectional excitement ran highest, risked his popularity and political prospects by supporting the compromise measures of 1850, in the hope that they would be respected and maintained throughout the Union as a final settlement of the slavery question, and thus reseal, as it were, the compact of union between all the States.

It required a devotion to the Union like that which animated Mr. Cobb, it required a mind which could rise above the region of local and sectional prejudices and view the interests of the whole Union with the eyes of a broad patriotism, and it required a boldness and firmness which nothing but a consciousness of right and an enlightened sense of duty can impart, to assume the responsibility of the part which he took in the passage of the compromise measures in opposition to most of his political friends and associates, and in opposition to the then prevalent sentiments of the Southern people.

He believed that a faithful acquiescence in and observance of the terms of the compromise measures would for ever settle the vexed question between the two sections; and he further believed that they did not involve the surrender of any practical right in which the honor and interest of the South were concerned.

When these measures were adopted, Mr. Cobb was Speaker of the House of Representatives, to which elevated and responsible position he was elected in December, 1849. During the six years of his service in Congress previous to his election as Speaker he had won great distinction by his ability, integrity, boldness and oratorical power, and had become the recognized leader of the Democratic party in the popular branch of the Federal legislature. From the beginning of his Congressional career, although he made no effort to attract attention, and only took such a part in the debates as his duty as a Representative seemed to demand, he was regarded by all parties as one of the ablest among the many able men who then adorned the lower House of Congress; and his thorough knowledge of parliamentary law and of the rules of Congress gave him a great advantage over those who were less conversant with this important branch of forensic science. He was a strong and earnest partisan because he had a deep-rooted faith in the principles and policy of the Democratic party, but in his intercourse with the members and in the interchanges of the amenities and courtesies of society he secured the good-will and friendship even of those who politically were most bitterly hostile to him. In the Thirtieth Congress, during which the Mexican war was the principal subject of discussion, and President Polk was violently attacked by the opposition on account of his policy in regard to it, Mr. Cobb took a prominent part in the debates, and proved himself to be one of the most effective defenders of the Administration. No member of the Democratic party in the House stood higher in the esteem and confidence of the President and his Cabinet than he did, and during Mr. Polk's term of office, on all important questions, he invariably sought the advice of the gifted young Representative of the Sixth District of Georgia, who had then acquired the distinction of being the acknowledged leader of his party.

In 1848, after the close of the Mexican war, the Presidential canvass, resulting in the election of General Taylor and the defeat of the Democratic party, placed Mr. Cobb in opposition. He had been the strenuous supporter of General Cass for the Presidency, and had taken an active part in the campaign. The tenure of substantial power by the Whigs was destined to be of short duration. When

Congress met in 1849, eight months after the inauguration of President Taylor, the Whig party was already rent asunder by dissensions and differences in its own ranks. It had a nominal majority of a few votes in the House of Representatives, but as a party it was powerless, owing to the irreconcilable difference between the Northern and Southern Whigs upon the slavery question. These same differences existed also among the Democrats, and consequently the country was agitated and disturbed to an alarming degree. It was under these circumstances that, after a most exciting contest, Howell Cobb of Georgia was elected Speaker.

The trust was high, the tribute to his ability and integrity which it conveyed was most flattering, but the position was as trying and responsible as can well be conceived, when it is remembered that his own party was not united, that the executive department of the government was held by the opposition, and that the agitation of the slavery question had almost reached the point of open warfare.

With a reliance on the integrity of his purpose, and on his determination to discharge his duty fully and impartially, he assumed the office; and it was universally admitted by all parties that the Speaker's chair was never filled by any one who had performed its duties more ably, impartially and patiently, or more acceptably to the House and to the country. Had he possessed less of the boldness, conservatism, good temper and honesty which characterized his whole life, he could not have exercised the persuasive power which he did in the peaceful settlement of the troubles which then existed, and in the reconciliation of those whose hostility was such that they were prepared to resort to the *ultima ratio* of republics as well as of kings. It is undoubtedly true that the passage of the compromise measures was largely due to the energy and influence of Mr. Cobb, although his position as Speaker prevented his taking as prominent a part in the debates as many others who appear to have contributed more directly to their adoption.

The Southern Rights party were bitterly opposed to the compromise, insisted that it was inconsistent with the honor and interests of the Southern States, and assailed all those Southern Representatives, especially Howell Cobb, who had been instrumental in its passage.

The consequence was, that Mr. Cobb, when he returned to Georgia after the adjournment of Congress, found himself compelled to vindicate his conduct and to defend himself against the assaults that were made upon him by former friends and associates. Conscious of the entire rectitude of his course, sustained by a sense of patriotic duty performed, and determined, at whatever cost of popularity or future political position, to maintain the settlement which he believed to be wise and for the welfare of the Union, he met the attack with unfaltering boldness.

Upon the issue on this question between the Southern Rights party and the Union party of Georgia, Mr. Cobb was nominated by the latter as their candidate for the office of governor of his State against the Hon. Charles J. McDonald, the candidate of the Southern Rights party. The canvass was one of unusual bitterness and excitement. Mr. Cobb made speeches in every county in Georgia, and wherever he spoke he vindicated his conduct with such powerful effect and convincing eloquence that when the day of election closed he was chosen governor of Georgia by the largest majority ever given in the State.

Governor Cobb's administration of the State government gave great satisfaction to all classes of the people. His messages to the Legislature were remarkably able, and by his wise selection of the proper agents the Western and Atlantic Railroad, from Atlanta to Chattanooga, which is the property of the State and a rich source of revenue, was raised to a high degree of efficiency and of profit. When he vacated the governor's chair in 1852, at the end of the term for which he was elected, he returned to his home in Athens, Ga., and resumed the practice of his profession. Beyond taking an active part in the Presidential campaign of 1852 in support of General Franklin Pierce, he remained in private life until 1855, when he was again called by the electors of his old district, whose affection and confidence had never deserted him, to serve them again in Congress.

In the mean time, the differences and animosities which were caused by the compromise of 1850 and the gubernatorial contest had in a great measure passed away. The Democratic party had again become united at the Baltimore Convention. The platform of principles promulgated by that body had endorsed the compromise measures, and thus Mr. Cobb found his conduct approved by the sound and mature judgment of those who two years before had denounced him for having surrendered the rights of the South.

The Thirty-fourth Congress, in which the Democratic party was greatly in the minority, was the last in which he served in the Federal legislature. His talents, his great parliamentary skill and his eminent social virtues gave him great weight in the House of Representatives; and though the spirit of hostility between the Republicans of the North and the Representatives from the South had become very angry and demonstrative during the last years of Mr. Pierce's administration, those who occupied seats in Congress at that time will remember how few there were who did not feel kindly and admiringly toward Howell Cobb. In the Presidential contest of 1856, Mr. Cobb took the stump in several of the Northern States in support of his personal and political friend, Mr. Buchanan; and when, after his election, which he owed in so great a measure to the efforts of Mr. Cobb, Mr Buchanan tendered him the position of Secretary of State, Mr. C. declined that position in favor of General Cass, and accepted the post of Secretary of the Treasury.

While Mr. Cobb continued in Mr. Buchanan's

Cabinet, from March, 1857, to December, 1860, it is within the personal knowledge of the writer of this sketch that he enjoyed the unbounded confidence and intimate personal friendship of the President, and occupied closer relations toward him than any other member of his Cabinet. Although General Cass was nominally the head of the Cabinet, and though he was respected and venerated by the President and by his colleagues as well for his great ability as for his long life of distinguished public service, his great age and feeble health often incapacitated him for the active discharge of his duties, and Mr. Cobb was really the prime minister of the Administration.

It is not within the purpose of this sketch to review the events of the Presidency of Mr. Buchanan, or to evoke discussion by making prominent and particular reference to the part which Mr. Cobb bore in the history of that time. The sectional contest which culminated in revolution and the greatest war of modern times toward the close of Mr. Buchanan's term of office is too fresh in the recollection of both parties to the contest—the wounds which it has caused are not yet sufficiently healed—to justify the hope that public opinion will deal impartially and calmly with the acts of those prominent men whose sense of patriotic duty impelled them to become leaders of the revolution. Mr. Cobb undoubtedly was one of the most prominent leaders of the revolution. His voice and influence certainly caused Georgia to follow the example of South Carolina, and sever her connection with the Federal Union. Had he advised otherwise or had he been silent, it is universaliy believed that Georgia would not have seceded when she did; and had she declined to secede, or even had she hesitated, it is also universally believed that the other States would not have seceded.

The contrast has been drawn by unfriendly, hostile critics with a view to damage the reputation of Mr. Cobb between his conduct in support of the compromise measures in 1850 and in defence of the Union and the course which he pursued in 1860–'61 in support of secession and in advocacy of a dissolution of the Union. Unworthy motives of selfishness and disappointed ambition have been imputed to him as the cause of his alleged change of sentiment; and even in the announcement of his sudden death, before the grave had closed over him, partisan violence and animosity were so strong and bitter that these charges were repeated when most men observe the accepted rule, *De mortuis nil nisi bonum.*

However men may differ from him in the course which he pursued, or however they may deny that the circumstances warranted the secession of the Southern States, those who knew Mr. Cobb, were familiar with the character and the principles which regulated his life, know that his motives were purely patriotic, and that when he counseled the Southern States to separate from the rest of the Federal family after the election of Abraham Lincoln had proclaimed the triumph of the platform of the Republican party, he did so because he believed that it was necessary for the preservation of the rights and liberties of his State and section, because he believed that argument, protest and remonstrance had been used in vain, and because he believed, as he expressed it in his address to the people of Georgia, written immediately after he resigned the office of Secretary of the Treasury (December 6, 1860), that "the Union formed by our fathers, which was one of equality, justice and fraternity, would be supplanted on the 4th of March, 1860, by a Union of sectionalism and hatred—the one worthy of the support and devotion of freemen, the other only possible at the cost of Southern honor, safety and independence." His address, in which his views and convictions are fully set forth as the basis of his counsel to the people of Georgia, will be fresh in the recollection of those who remember the history of that eventful period, and it is unnecessary to reproduce it here. Mr. Cobb recommended secession because he thought it was the only means of defence left to the people of the slaveholding States, and he justified it on the grounds upon which the right of revolution is justified, with a full knowledge of the dangers and difficulties by which its exercise is surrounded. Nor is there any inconsistency, as heated partisans pretend, between his course in 1850 and that which he adopted in 1860. The circumstances by which he was surrounded when he supported the compromise measures were widely different from those which existed when he told the people of Georgia that there was "no other remedy for the existing state of things but immediate secession." He advocated the compromise measures because he believed that they would be faithfully observed by both sections as a final settlement of the vexed question of slavery, without any loss of honor or practical right on the part of the South; and he advocated secession because that basis of settlement had been ignored and set aside, because he saw, as Mr. Seward expressed it during the canvass of 1860, that "the time had come at last when the South was not only powerless, but without influence in the government," that the executive, legislative and judicial departments of the government were about to pass into the hands of men whose avowed policy was hostile to the rights, prejudicial to the interests and insulting to the honor of the Southern States. His attachment to the "Union formed by our fathers" was unchanged, and he only consented to its dissolution because he was convinced that its continuance would be the ruin of his own section.

As his friend, Hon. Philip Clayton, remarked in this connection, in a letter to the editor of this volume written shortly after General Cobb's death, "the man who has enjoyed the security and luxury of his quiet home, around whose associations every tendril of his heart has been entwined, is not and cannot be accused of inconsistency when the devouring element forces him to leave all he holds dear and seek safety under some other shelter.

So with General Cobb. He gave up the government of his affections because it was in flames, and sought another where he believed he could ultimately find repose and safety."

Indeed, General Cobb was naturally and eminently conservative in character, taste and habit. He was a man of peace, and his heart ever beat for peace and repose. In 1850 he was for compromise, because he was for peace; in 1860 he was for secession, for the same reason—because he was for peace. He believed that the compromise measures of 1850 would restore harmony to the entire country; therefore he advocated them. When he found that they totally failed to allay the storm of sectional passion, and to bring the North and South into repose upon the Constitution of the fathers, he saw that in the Union there could be no peace—that the institution of domestic slavery, with which he had been raised and which he approved, would be a growing cause of irritation and excitement year by year unless abandoned by the South. He believed that institution to have been guaranteed and protected by the Constitution of the fathers; he was not prepared to sacrifice it for the Union; and he saw in secession and a division of the country the only other solution of the difficulties by which the country was imperiled and its peace threatened.

Therefore he advocated secession as a measure of peace, of true conservatism; and had the counsels of peace rendered by such men as General Scott and Horace Greeley prevailed, there would have been no difficulty in reconciling his conduct in 1850 and 1860. Loving the Union, he tried to preserve it with slavery as a domestic institution secured to his section, so long as he saw the slightest hope of preserving both in peace. Loving that section and that institution more than the Union, he saw in secession the only hope of their peaceful preservation.

The war came, and before its rude breath the best calculations of statesmanship and philosophy were swept away; yet reason with unclouded vision sees the clear sky beyond the storm-cloud, and reconciles the mind and heart of the Howell Cobb of 1850 with the mind and heart of the same man in 1860. Both toiled and beat for peace and conservatism in the one case as in the other, and the unyielding Union man of 1850 is one and the same with the uncompromising secessionist of 1860.

Conservative he was when he left Georgia for Congress in 1842—conservative throughout his Congressional career—conservative in the gubernatorial struggle of 1850, and not less so, parodoxical as it may have seemed to the carnal thinker, nôt less conservative in his effort to separate his section from a Union which promised no more of peace to him and to his.

The writer of this sketch has not dwelt upon this portion of Mr. Cobb's career with any view to apologize for his conduct or to attempt to reconcile its apparent inconsistency with a previous portion of his public life, but to vindicate the truthfulness of his character and the patriotic integrity of his motives, so well known to all who were associated with him in 1860–'61, and to none better than to him who writes these pages.

After he had resigned his seat in Mr. Buchanan's Cabinet, Mr. Cobb issued the address to the people of Georgia—to which reference has been already made—and immediately returned to his State to place his services at the disposal of his people.

In the canvass for the election of delegates to the Convention of Georgia, which adopted the ordinance of secession, Mr. Cobb bore a prominent and influential part. He made public speeches in various parts of the State, and earnestly recommended secession as the only means of safety. Although he was not a member of that Convention, with that commanding eloquence which was part of his intellectual character, he contributed in no small degree to the adoption of the ordinance by which it was declared that "the Union subsisting between the State of Georgia and other States under the name of the United States of America was dissolved, and that the State of Georgia was in the full possession and exercise of all those rights of sovereignty which belong and appertain to a free and independent State."

This step once taken, it was immediately followed by the States of Alabama, Mississippi, Florida, Louisiana and Texas; and delegates were elected by the seceded States to a convention to meet in Montgomery, Ala., on the 4th of February, 1861, for the purpose of forming a government and framing a constitution for a Southern confederacy. When this convention met, Mr. Cobb was unanimously chosen to be its president. With the acts and deliberations of that body, subsequently strengthened and increased by the accession of representatives from the States of Tennessee, Arkansas, North Carolina and Virginia, and still later by representatives from Kentucky and Missouri, all are familiar. This is not the place, nor is it the design of this volume, to detail the events which led to the formation of the Confederate States of America as an independent republic; nor those subsequent events which constitute the terrible drama of 1861–5, of which the Southern States were the theatre, except in so far as the subject of this memoir is immediately connected with them.

When it became evident that the government and people of the United States were resolved to prevent the secession of the Southern States and the formation of a Southern republic by force of arms, and that war was inevitable, Mr. Cobb felt it to be his duty to share the dangers of the battlefield with those who were exposed to them by following his advice.

In the summer of 1861 he raised a regiment of volunteers, known as the Sixteenth Georgia Regiment, and as one of the most gallant and distinguished organizations in the Confederate army, and assumed command as colonel. During the fall and winter of 1861 he served with his regiment on that portion of Tidewater Virginia known as the Peninsula, under the immediate command of General J. B. Magruder; and in the spring of 1862, having been promoted to the command of a brigade, bore a distinguished part in that series of engagements which took place between the United States forces under General McClellan and General Magruder's small force, by which the Federal troops were successfully held in check until General J. E. Johnston assumed command and decided to evacute the Peninsula and concentrate the Confederate forces in front of Richmond.

In the engagement at Dam No. 1, on the Warwick River, where the United States forces made repeated attempts to cross the stream and break through the Confederate lines, General Cobb was in immediate command of the Confederate troops at that point, and won deserved distinction for the victory which was gained by his command. In General Magruder's report of that battle the gallantry of General Cobb's command and the skillful dispositions of the commander are mentioned in terms of marked commendation.

On the formation of the permanent government of the Confederate States, February 22, 1862,

General Cobb's duties as president of the Provincial Congress terminated. Thenceforward he gave all his time and energies to the military service; and from the retreat to Richmond from the Peninsula to the close of the first campaign in Maryland after the battle of Sharpsburg, including the memorable battles of the Seven Pines, the Seven Days' Fights from Mechanicsville to Malvern Hill, the Second Battle of Manassas, the capture of Harper's Ferry, Crampton Gap and Sharpsburg, he and his brigade were always present and always conspicuous for their gallantry and good discipline.

At the battle of Crampton Gap, where, owing to a careless reconnoisance of the enemy's position and strength by the Confederate cavalry, and by a recklessly conjectural report of the force in his front, General Cobb's brigade, finding itself opposed to General Franklin's entire corps, was compelled to retreat, and suffered heavy losses in killed and wounded, among the former of whom were his brother-in-law, Colonel John B. Lamar, the only brother of Mrs. Cobb, who was serving on his personal staff, and his cousin, Lieutenant-Colonel Jefferson Lamar, commanding the infantry battalion of the Cobb Legion, nothing but General Cobb's coolness, presence of mind and rapidity of action, could have saved the brigade from annihilation. Had such a calamity occurred, the whole responsibility would have rested with the general of cavalry, who said to General Cobb, as he went forward, "You have nothing but a brigade in your front, sir."

After the termination of the campaign of 1862, pressing family business compelled him to obtain leave of absence to return to Georgia, at the expiration of which the Confederate Government, deeming his popular influence of great importance in the settlement of differences which had begun to appear between the State and the Confederate authorities in the rapid recruitment of the army and the efficient contribution of supplies, assigned him to the command of the Military District of Florida, and subsequently, having promoted him to the rank of major-general, to the command of the District of Georgia and of the reserve forces of that State; which latter command he held until the close of the war, when, after the unequal and sanguinary battle of Columbus, having learned of the surrender of Generals Lee and Johnston, he surrendered at Macon, Ga., to Major-General Wilson, commanding a division of United States cavalry.

Although his habits, tastes, mode of life, early training and inclinations unfitted him for the camp and the profession of a soldier, the same sense of duty, steadfastness of purpose, intellectual quickness and determination to succeed in whatever he attempted, distinguished him in his military as in his civil career. From the moment he determined to enter the army he devoted himself to the study of tactics, drill and the routine duties of a soldier with all the zeal and assiduity of a recruit, and with astonishing rapidity became such a perfect master of the art that his command soon became distinguished in the army for its thorough drill and discipline. He was personally beloved by all his officers and men. While he was firm in the enforcement of all military regulations and implicit obedience to orders, he was untiring in his efforts to provide for their wants and comforts, sharing all their privations and perils, and never asking them to do what he was not ready to do himself. To his superiors in military rank he yielded as ready obedience as any private in the ranks. This example, so valuable in a volunteer army, his ready and intelligent performance of duty, his mature judgment in council and his genial nature as a companion, won him the respect, confidence and attached friendship of all those under whose command he served.

After the struggle was over, and the cause which he had served so zealously was for ever lost, faithful to the terms of his parole as to every other obligation, he did much by his precept and example to promote the quiet disbandment of the Confederate army, and the return of the soldiers to the peaceful pursuits of life. This accomplished, he withdrew to his home in Athens, Ga., where he had been but for a short time, when an order was sent by the War Department to General Wilson to arrest him and send him to Washington City. Much against his will, General Wilson obeyed the order, which was a violation of the express letter of the parole which he had taken from General Cobb; and whether in consequence of General Wilson's remonstrance, or of a better perception by the War Department of the force of their obligations to paroled officers, when General Cobb reached Nashville in custody of a United States officer he was released by orders from Washington.

He returned at once to Georgia, and having formed a partnership with his near relative and lifelong friend, Hon. James Jackson, he opened a law-office in Macon, and determined to devote himself to the practice of his profession. Although for many years he had practically, though not formally, retired from the Bar, from the moment he resumed his place he and his partner did an extensive practice in the circuits of South-western and Middle Georgia, and many of the most important cases in the Supreme Court of the State were confided to his management. There was no more assiduous student, no more careful and painstaking attorney in the preparation of cases, no more faithful and conscientious advocate, than General Cobb; and whether in a close, logical, strong, concise argument of a difficult question of law before the Supreme Court, or in an impassioned address to a jury in defence of a prisoner, General Cobb, it is admitted, had few rivals and no superior among the Bar of Georgia. The venerable and lamented Chief-Justice, Joseph Henry Lumpkin, told the writer on his return home at the end of a term of the Supreme Court, during which General Cobb had argued against the constitutionality of a stay law, on the ground that such a law impairs the validity of contracts, that never in all his experience at the Bar and on the Bench had he heard a finer argument than that of General Cobb. His professional speeches were always plain, terse, strong and directly to the point. He rarely used ornament, and never indulged in far-fetched illustration. His power consisted in the plainness and candor of his propositions, in his thorough mastery of the law, in his rapid perception of the points of his case, and in the earnestness and energy of his manner. No man was ever more respectful to others, no one was ever more kind and considerate toward his juniors. While he always bore himself with dignity, and never violated decorum, he was seldom severe, and never supercilious or overbearing.

But better and more valuable testimony than can be derived from any other source in regard to General Cobb's career as a lawyer, is given in another part of this volume by the eminent members of the Bar at which he practiced, who assembled after his death to record their appreciation of his worth and their sorrow at his loss. With many of those distinguished men he had been associated during his entire public career. To many of them he had been opposed in politics. To all he had been known, whether at the Bar, in the political arena or in the intimacy of social life; and it is not extravagant to say that by all he was admired and respected for his undoubted genius and commanding talent, by all he was reverenced for his high character, spotless integrity and unsullied honor, and by all he was beloved for his winning manners, genial intercourse and attractive conversation.

For many years he had taken a deep interest in the education of the youth of his State, and as a trustee of the University of Georgia took a zealous and active part in all the measures of improvement and reform by which that institution has been raised to its present high position among the most prominent educational establishments in the United States. On this subject, too, the reader is referred to the action of the Board of Trustees of the University on the announcement of his death.

But great as Howell Cobb undoubtedly was as a statesman, orator, lawyer and public man, as a private citizen, as the head of a family, as a friend, he was still greater and more admirable. Possessed of large means, he used them to promote the happiness and comfort of all around him. No applicant for help or charity ever applied to him in vain; and it is only since his death, since the grateful recipients of his bounty, in expressing their grief at the irreparable loss they have sustained, have made known the benefits they have received at his hands, that the extent and liberality of his charities have become known. He seemed to act upon the Christian rule, never to let his right hand know what his left hand did. In every public charity, in the building and endowment of places of Christian worship, in the promotion of schools and colleges, in the aid of every good and useful work, he was always ready to contribute liberally.

He was a large slave-owner. When by the result of the war the slaves were emancipated, more than a thousand negroes called him master. A more liberal, indulgent or kind master never lived. When he died all of his old servants who could do so attended his funeral, and there were but few more sincere and afflicted mourners at his grave than those negroes. Although relieved by emancipation from all obligation to provide for any of his former slaves, he supported during his life, and his family still support, all of his servants who from age, disease or other infirmity were unable to provide for themselves. All have good houses, ample food and fuel, comfortable clothing and medical care; and whenever he visited the places where they live, he always took care to see that these pensioners were comfortable.

In a former part of this sketch his character and example as the head of a family have been noticed. It was in his own house, surrounded by his family, that he was most to be admired. His chief aim in life was to secure the happiness of those who were related to him; and amid all the stirring events of his career he never allowed any consideration of personal pleasure or ambition to induce him to postpone even for a moment what he owed to his family.

In illustration of this admirable trait of his character, it may not be deemed inappropriate to mention an incident of his early life which will exhibit the unselfishness of his nature and the readiness with which he could sacrifice his own interest to protect that of a relative. While he was quite young he endorsed notes to a very large amount for his father, Colonel John A. Cobb, who was then engaged in land speculations to a great extent. Overtaken by the great commercial panic of 1837, when lands and every other species of property depreciated so rapidly in value, Colonel Cobb failed for a large amount; and after all his property had been sold at the then low prices to satisfy his creditors, there still remained a considerable sum unpaid, for which his son Howell was liable as endorser. Although legally and equitably he could have evaded the payment of these claims, and though their payment would not only involve the loss of a handsome estate bequeathed to him by his uncle, Captain Howell Cobb, but embarrass him very seriously for many years, and though he had never derived any personal benefit from any of the transactions on which he was held liable, he resolutely refused to avail himself of any means to escape liability, and paid all the claims to the uttermost farthing, principal and interest; and thus during several years of his life was in straitened circumstances.

General Cobb never made any open profession of religion by connecting himself formally with any church. But no man admired religion or a religious life more than he, and no man ever prayed more devoutly to receive the light of life. For many years he had been beset by doubts as to some essential points of the Christian religion. He struggled hard to dissipate his doubts, and in his discussions with ministers of the gospel with whom he was intimate, and with attached friends, he frankly stated his difficulties and sought for aid to remove them. He was a constant and devout worshiper at the Baptist church, and his private devotions were never forgotten. A few months before his death, in conversation with a devoted personal friend, he mentioned his religious troubles and his anxiety to remove them. His friend, who had experienced similar difficulties, and had had them removed by reading a little book, "The Christ of History," by Dr. John Young, recommended him to read it, and the result was the entire removal of his skepticism, and a perfect belief in all the saving doctrines of Christianity. He had resolved, on his return to Macon from a contemplated visit to the North with a portion of his family, to connect himself with the Church. His death at New York, on the 9th of October, 1868, prevented the execution of this purpose; but in a conversation between him and the bishop of Georgia, Dr. Beckwith, in the course of which he was stricken down and never spoke again, he made a full profession of his faith in the Christian religion, and died with that profession still on his lips.

During the past few months of his life, from having had an iron constitution impervious to disease, he suffered frequently from a painful oppression of the chest and the region of the heart, which caused much anxiety to his family and friends. But his malady was not considered dangerous, and no cause of immediate alarm was felt.

The evening previous to his departure from his home in Georgia to the North, he passed in company with a few friends, among whom was the writer of these pages. He never appeared in better health or spirits, and none of those who were present when they parted from him dreamed that they would never again behold him in life. On the morning of his death he was, to all appearance, in the enjoyment of excellent health. He had just returned to New York from a visit to Niagara, Saratoga and other points of interest, and had made his arrangements to return to Georgia, when, as he stood conversing with Bishop Beckwith and Col. J. J. Williams of Florida, formerly of his staff, and with his wife and daughter standing near, he was stricken with apoplexy, and died almost immediately. He was exactly fifty-three years one month and two days old at the time of his death.

His remains were transported to Georgia, and were interred in the family vault in Athens, in presence of an immense concourse of people from Athens and other parts of the State.

Besides his widow, he has left four sons—namely, Captain John A. Cobb, Major Lamar Cobb, Captain Howell Cobb and Andrew Jackson Cobb; and three daughters—Miss Mary Ann Lamar Cobb, Miss Sarah Cobb and Miss Lizzie Craig Cobb. To them, and to those who were intimately associated with him in private life, his death is an irreparable loss. But there are consolations which arise to mitigate their loss, and soothe the sharp pangs of sorrow by the healing balm of resignation. They are grateful to God that he lived so long, that he did so much and so well for his family, his friends and his country, and that his great name is so honorably connected with that country's records. They are grateful that he has left upon their minds and hearts an ineffaceable impression of his person, his character and his public acts. They are grateful that they have seen and known him; and when they in their turn shall be called hence to be no more seen, they will take with them an enduring sense of his virtues, his honor, his blameless life and his lovable nature.

William M. Browne.

Howell Cobb

HON. HOWELL COBB.

DEATH.

All flesh shall perish together, and man shall turn again into dust.—Job xxxiv. 15.

Then shall the earth return unto the dust as it was: and the spirit shall return unto God who gave it.—Ecclesiastes xii. 7.

Let me die the death of the righteous, and let my last end be like his!—Numbers xxiii. 10.

Precious in the sight of the Lord is the death of his saints.—Psalm cxvi. 15.

O death, where is thy sting? O grave, where is thy victory? The sting of death is sin; and the strength of sin is the law. But thanks be to God, which giveth us the victory, through our Lord Jesus Christ.—1 Corinthians xv. 55, 56, 57.

Lo! the prisoner is released,
  Lightened of his fleshly load;
Where the weary are at rest,
  He is gathered unto God!
Lo! the pain of life has past,
  All his warfare now is o'er;
Death and hell behind are cast,
  Grief and suffering are no more.

Death comes to take me where I long to be;
  One pang, and bright blooms the immortal flower;
Death comes to lead me from mortality
  To lands which know not one unhappy hour;
I have a hope, a faith—from sorrow here
I'm led by Death away—why should I start and fear?

HON. HOWELL COBB.

I.

DEATH.

N the 9th of October, 1868, the following dispatch winged its way, with lightning speed, from the city of New York to Georgia:

NEW YORK, October 9, 1868.

To DAVID C. BARROW, *Athens*, *Ga.:*

Gen'l Cobb died suddenly this morning.

(Signed) R. D. MOORE, M. D.

The mournful news thrilled the heart of the entire State with a pang of grief. Never before had a son of Georgia passed away whose death brought more general sorrow, and whose untimely end created a more poignant regret. Although the State had lost many whose death she deplored with heartfelt anguish, as was the case when the spirit of the venerated Elliott winged its sudden flight to the realms of bliss; or when the peerless Lumpkin sank to rest in the bosom of his God; or when the beloved T. R. R. Cobb rose to glory from the ensanguined field; yet, never before had she lost one who enjoyed her confidence and love in a greater degree, and whose eminent abilities and prudence as a statesman she so greatly needed.

It may be truly said of Gov. Cobb that, at the time of his death, no man in the State possessed so many friends, or stood higher in the estimation of all as a high-toned, honorable Southern gentleman.

He was a man universally respected and admired for his ardent patriotism, for his lofty abilities, for his noble qualities of head and heart, for his unbounded hospitality and generosity, and for his courteous demeanor and incorruptible integrity. His was truly a princely nature—above all meanness, staunch in its friendships, unwavering in its constancy, unfaltering in its devotion; to the last degree generous and unselfish, self-sacrificing in the interests of family, friends and country, and sublime in its contempt and loathing of all that was base and hypocritical. No man ever endeared himself more to loved ones, or would more willingly have benefited an enemy. To a towering intellect he united a warm and tender nature; and to a mind that had swayed a nation he united the humble spirit of a Christian. His heart beat in unison with the great pulse of our common humanity, and all the impulses of his nature manifested a sympathy for friends and country that no circumstances could weaken or destroy. To whatever post assigned he had proved himself faithful, and in whatever capacity employed he had manifested his ability. No taint ever attached to his name: no suspicion ever tarnished his character. From his first entrance into public life, his State had delighted to honor him, and never once had she seen cause to blush for her confidence or feel abased by her affection.

And when he died she mourned for him as for a favorite son. She covered herself with sackcloth and wept, for she knew that his like would not be seen again.

With his wife and daughter he had gone to New York on a pleasure trip. The full strength of mature and vigorous manhood was in his frame, and, to all appearances, he bade fair to live long in the enjoyment of honors, wealth and fame; and yet in a moment he was smitten down by the hand of death, and expired without a groan.

The particulars of his death may be briefly told. He was standing on the parlor floor of the Fifth Avenue Hotel, conversing with the Right Rev. Bishop Beckwith in relation to a sermon preached by the latter. Major Joseph John Williams, of Florida, a former member of Gen. Cobb's staff, was present also, and writes as follows concerning the sad event:

"As we were about parting at the head of the stairs on the parlor floor, Mrs. Cobb and Miss Mary Cobb made their appearance, descending. The General asked the Bishop to remain and be introduced. He did so, and Mrs. Cobb and the Bishop immediately commenced conversation upon the same subject. The General, standing just to my left, quickly threw his hand to his head, walked around and took his seat upon the stairs, and in a very few minutes expired, without saying a word."

The great man had seen his last of earth.

The last conversation Gen. Cobb had on earth was with the Right Rev. Bishop Beckwith, of

Georgia, at the Fifth Avenue Hotel, New York City. An account of that conversation and the accompanying interview will prove exceedingly interesting. It is furnished by Bishop Beckwith himself:

Gov. Cobb's Last Conversation.

"Rev. and Dear Sir: On the morning of the 9th day of October, 1868, being in the city of New York, I visited the Fifth Avenue Hotel, where I accidentally met my old friend and schoolmate, Col. Joseph John Williams, of Florida. In the course of conversation he informed me that Gen. Howell Cobb (upon whose staff he had served during the war) was in the hotel, and proposed that I should call upon him, saying that the General had heard me preach a sermon in Macon, Georgia, of which he had spoken in terms of strong condemnation. Col. Williams declared his belief that the General had misunderstood me, and desired me to offer him an explanation. Glad of an opportunity, I consented, and we went in search of him, little dreaming what we were to hear and see. We found the General standing near the doors of the parlors, in conversation with some ladies. When disengaged, the Colonel and myself approached, and, after the usual exchange of courtesies, I remarked to him that I had understood he had censured a sermon preached by me in Macon upon Christian Unity; begged him to state his objections and give me the opportunity of removing them. He very kindly and frankly declared that he did object to that sermon, upon the ground that he understood it to contain *two* statements: 1, That I did not believe a Baptist could be saved; and 2, That I had placed Baptists (who believe in the Lord's divinity) upon an equality with Unitarians. I assured him that in each case he had entirely misunderstood both my statements and my opinions. As to the first, I said, there is not a word in the sermon which can be made to mean anything of the kind; and more than that, I do not hold such opinion. I added, that I believed the Baptist Church—as a system—contained very grave errors, but I did not believe that the members of that Church would therefore be lost. I acknowledged their piety and devotion, and believed that numbers of them—as of the other churches—would be saved. He answered,

"'Had you only said you expected to see Baptists in heaven, all would have been right.' I replied,

"'I did not *say* so, because it did not occur to me that I *could* be suspected of holding any other opinion.' He said, warmly and frankly, that he had misunderstood me; and during the conversation he more than once recurred to the above statement, and thanked me for having made it. I told him that I had heard of this his charge against my sermon before, and had consequently made inquiry of others, and invariably received the answer that they were surprised that he could have so understood me. As to Objection 2d, I said, 'In showing the sad *results* of irresponsible private judgment, I had mentioned the fact that one denomination (the Quakers) denied visible sacraments; another (the Baptists) refused baptism to infants, and allowed the holy communion only to such as had been immersed; another (the Universalists) denied eternal punishment; another (the Unitarians) denied the Lord's divinity; and several denied the three orders of the ministry; but that I *did not* institute *any comparison* between them. The idea of placing the Unitarian—who denies the Lord's divinity—upon an equality with the Baptist—who believes in it—did not once occur to me.' He saw his mistake at once, frankly confessed that he was wrong, and hesitated not to say he was surprised that he should have so misunderstood me.

"He then said, 'Your argument against private judgment is one that I cannot see how it can be answered.' He then told me that he had long desired to connect himself with some Church; he felt it to be his duty to do so.

"'But,' said he, 'none of you will have me. You will not have me, because I do not believe in the apostolic succession; and the Baptists will not have me, because I do not believe any of their doctrines.'

"I said, 'We do not require belief in the apostolic succession as a term of communion; we believe that we have that succession, but do not refuse communion to those who do not believe it.'

"He said, 'I had a talk with my minister some time since, and told him that I wished to join the Church; that the Baptist Church was my Church, and the Church of my people, but I did not believe in the necessity of immersion, nor in their doctrine of election.' I asked what was the reply of the minister; my memory is not positive as to his answer; the impression upon my mind is to the effect that he said his minister would not consent to receive him. (The minister can correct this if it be necessary.)*

* Rev. S. Boykin—Dear Brother: On page 7 of the paper you handed to me on the death of Gov. Cobb, prepared by Bishop Beckwith, he quotes this language from the Governor: "I had a talk with my minister some time since, and told him that I wished to join the Church; that the Baptist Church was my Church, and the Church of my people, but I did not believe in the necessity of immersion, nor in their doctrine of election." The Bishop adds, "I asked what was the reply of the minister; my memory is not positive as to his answer; the impression upon my mind is to the effect that his minister would not consent to receive him. (The minister can correct this if it be necessary)."

The quotation from Gov. Cobb is doubtless in the main correct; much more was said, and explanations were given, but upon the two points of *immersion* and *election* I wish to add a word.

When Gov. Cobb said he did not believe immersion was necessary (the word he used was *essential*) to baptism, I asked why he did not—if he had ever seen where anything else was taught in the word of God for baptism? He said,

"I frankly confess to you, sir, I have not. I am only led to this conclusion by the great diversity of opinions entertained among learned and good men. I believe something else may do, because they say it will." I said to him,

"We take the Bible for our guide. We adopt its teachings as the rule of our practice; and while we award much learning and piety to men, we search the Scriptures and bring every man's theory to this inspired test, and accept or reject it as it may accord with, or differ from, God's revealed will. We will receive you upon this principle; and give you permission to withdraw from our communion whenever you shall be convinced that the Bible teaches anything for baptism but immersion. But we will not expect

"Immediately after this he said that for some time past he had been very much troubled by a matter which he considered of far more importance than the question of apostolic succession, etc. I asked if I might know what it was, and he answered with much feeling,

"'The divinity of our Lord.' He said that no one knew how it had troubled him and how much he had suffered. I think I can never forget his agitation as he thus unburdened his heart to me. I saw that the great trial of his life was before

you to inveigh against our doctrines or practices while a member of the Church!"

He then said, if his family were here he would join the Church immediately, and so soon as they returned from Athens he would do so.

He said he did not believe the doctrine of *election*. I asked him why?

"Because," said he, "I do not understand it."

"But," said I, "do you understand the mystery of godliness—God manifest in the flesh? You *believe* that, and yet you simply accept it on the divine veracity. Can you not believe the doctrine of election simply because it is taught in the Bible, even though you do not understand it? If it be a doctrine of the Bible (and you cannot deny that it is clearly taught), you are *bound to believe it*, or make God a liar. But you reverence him as the God of all truth and righteousness. Have you not reverence enough for the perfections of his character to believe all that he has revealed, whether it comes in antagonism with your own previous opinions or not?"

He replied with emphasis in the affirmative, and then the conversation turned upon his recent gracious experiences of the love of God in his soul.

E. W. WARREN,
Pastor First Baptist Church, Macon, Ga.

him: the memory of the pangs it had cost him seemed to affect him profoundly. I said,

"'General, have you overcome that difficulty?' He answered at once,

"'*I have.*'

"I said, 'Do you believe in the divinity of the Saviour?' I fancied there was something of joy in his prompt, decisive answer,

"'I do.'

"It was to me a moment of more than ordinary solemnity; and when I afterward thought of it, I felt, 'Surely the Lord had been in that place, and I knew it not.' That great intellect had met and struggled with infidelity as with a strong man armed; the effects of the strife were evident as he spoke; he seemed to feel that he had been rescued by an Omnipotent arm.

"I said, 'General, do you believe in the Apostles' Creed?' He paused, as though recalling its various articles, and then answered,

"'Yes, I do.'

"I then told him that he believed all that any Church had a right to demand as necessary to membership, and that I was ready to receive him into the Church, and give him the sacraments. He made no reply, but expressed a desire to introduce me to his wife, that he might correct her misapprehension of my sermon. As we moved to the stairway, we met Mrs. Cobb and her daughter coming down from their room. The introduction was given, the correction as to the sermon was made—and then the summons came. I feel, my dear sir, that I have no right to portray that scene or speak of its awful sufferings. Suffice it to say, that fifteen minutes had scarcely elapsed ere the strong man, with the confession of his Saviour before man still warm upon his lips, stood in that Saviour's presence.

"He was smitten down by apoplexy, and from the first moment was speechless.

"It would be unbecoming in me—a comparative stranger to Gen. Cobb—to speak of his public and private character: that privilege belongs to those who were permitted to know him well. God brought me into contact with him during the last—but most important—moments of his life. His labors in the Cabinet, the Senate and on the Field were all ended: life had reached its limit; and now, by circumstances seemingly accidental, an overruling Providence brought him to a minister of his Church, that he might open the grief of his soul and confess his Saviour before men. Some secret influence urged him to speak of the great trouble which had overshadowed his mind and tempted him "to deny the Lord that bought him." No man, my dear sir, can appreciate this trouble who has not felt it. It is the soul's struggle for life with its strongest, most insidious foe—Rationalism. By the mercy of God, Gen. Cobb had come out of that struggle victorious. Conscious now of his own weakness and constant need of divine aid, he desired to become a member of Christ's visible body, the Church, and to confess his Saviour before men. This desire he expressed to one of God's ministers; this confession he frankly and earnestly made; and even while he made it the message was received—'The master calleth for thee.'

"Most respectfully,

"Yours in Christ and his Church,

"JNO. W. BECKWITH."

When the sad event was known in Georgia, meetings of condolence were held throughout the State, and delegations were appointed to attend the funeral.

In various towns and cities the members of the Bar met and adopted resolutions significant of their sorrow, and expressive of their feelings of reverence and regard for the memory of their departed associate.

In Americus, Georgia, the following preamble and resolutions were adopted by the legal fraternity, and may serve as an exemplification to indicate the character of the meetings held, and the feelings and sentiments manifested, in other portions of the State:

In Memoriam of Hon. Howell Cobb.

Sumter Superior Court,
October Term, 1868.

HON. J. M. CLARK, PRESIDING.

The Committee appointed to report suitable preamble and resolutions of the Court and Bar, expressive of their sympathies arising from the sudden death of Hon. Howell Cobb, beg leave to submit the following:

The death of a prominent citizen is always a source of deep sorrow and regret. But when so distinguished a citizen as Hon. Howell Cobb is suddenly taken from the hope of his native State, we cannot but regard it as a great public calamity. Gov. Cobb, more perhaps than any man in the State, has a hold upon the hearts and confidence of the people. He had long served them in the national councils, in the Cabinet and as Governor; and in all the various and important public trusts he discharged his duties with distinguished ability, credit to himself and honor to his State. He was an eminent lawyer, and as a forensic speaker he had few equals and no superiors. In all the social relations of life he was affable, kind and courteous. His hospitality was unbounded. He had a large, generous and noble heart, filled with benevolent charity. An all-wise Providence has, we trust, taken him to Himself, and we submit with reverence to His holy will.

Georgia, in the death of our Cobb, has lost a favorite son. His seat in the court-room will never be filled again.

Resolved, That in the death of Hon. Howell Cobb, this State has lost one of its most eminent and distinguished citizens and statesmen, this Bar one of its ablest and most beloved members and the social circle one of its chief delights and ornaments; and that this Court and the members of this Bar feel the most poignant sorrow for the loss of the lamented dead.

Resolved, That we heartily condole with the bereaved family and friends of the deceased, and that his sudden death ought to admonish us all to be "ready also; for the Son of man cometh at an hour when we think not."

Resolved, That a copy of these proceedings be entered on the minutes of this Court, published in the city newspapers, and sent to the bereaved family of the deceased.

All of which is respectfully submitted.

Jas. J. Scarborough, Chairman.
Willis A. Hawkins,
N. A. Smith,
Charles T. Goode,
W. B. Guerry.

On motion, It was ordered that the proceedings be spread upon the minutes of this Court, and published in the city papers, and a certified copy sent to the bereaved family of Gov. Cobb.

J. M. Clark, J. S. C., S. W. C.

A true extract from the minutes of Sumter Superior Court, October 26, 1868.

A. J. Ronaldson, Clerk.

From the Columbian Bar emanated the following tribute of respect:

COLUMBUS, GEORGIA, October 10, 1868.

A public meeting was this day held in the city of Columbus, when, on motion, Gen. Henry L. Benning was called to the Chair, and Hugh King, Esq., appointed Secretary.

The Chairman announced that the startling and painful intelligence had reached us of the death of one of our purest, ablest and most patriotic men. Howell Cobb, the great Georgia statesman, had suddenly died in New York City, on the 9th inst., and this meeting had assembled to manifest our own feelings, as individuals, and to give expression to the loss which the country had sustained in this great calamity.

On motion, a committee of seven was appointed to draft resolutions expressive of the feelings of this meeting. Martin J. Crawford, A. R. Lamar, James N. Ramsey, Beverly A. Thornton, Alexander C. Morton Porter Ingram and F. G. Wilkins composed the committee. Whereupon the committee reported through Mr. Crawford, the following resolutions:

Resolved, That we have heard with the deepest

sensibility the announcement of the death of the Hon. Howell Cobb.

Resolved, That in his death this State and the country have indeed suffered an irreparable loss, and in sadness and sorrow we bow to this most painful and afflicting dispensation of an all-wise Providence.

Resolved, That this meeting tenders its heartfelt condolence and sympathy to the bereaved family of the deceased, and that, whilst we mingle our tears with theirs over the grave of the departed, we weep also because the wise and patriotic counsels of Howell Cobb are forever lost to his people.

Resolved, That a copy of the above resolutions be sent to the family of the deceased.

After beautiful and touching speeches, made by Messrs. Crawford, Ramsey, Lamar, Thornton, and Morton, the resolutions were adopted, and the meeting adjourned.

HENRY L. BENNING, Chairman.

HUGH KING, Secretary.

The entire press of the country did honor to the illustrious dead in words of eulogistic comment; but one extract only is made. It is an eloquent tribute to the memory of Gov. Cobb, taken from "Pensacola Commercial," and was written by Hon. Mr. Mallory, of Florida, who was associated with Mr. Cobb in official life, and appreciated his character and ability:

"The Southern heart will learn with profound regret the sudden and unlooked-for death of Howell Cobb.

"We do not write to praise the dead, but to manifest the grief of the living; and to speak this grief, so far as we may, for the people of Florida, in whose hearts his name and fame are enshrined with warm affection.

"Georgia does not mourn alone. Her grief is shared by sister States, who claim the genius, the services and the character of her son as the common property of the South, to which they have aided to give dignity and renown.

"Connected with him by ties which she can never forget; loved as he was in her every forest home; cherishing the principles he espoused and maintained with equal ardor and ability in field and forum, death could not have sent a shaft fraught with deeper sorrow to Florida than that which struck this noble Southerner; and in the hearts of her people will his epitaph be written.

"Our State has within a few dark years of suffering been called upon to mourn many whom she cherished in her heart of hearts; but over a purer spirit, a more lofty patriotism, a heart controlled by warmer affections, her tears have never fallen.

"The judgment of posterity reviews the deeds of those whom time submits to its scrutiny, uncontrolled by the opinions of their contemporaries; but when it pronounces upon the *man*, irrespective of station, it is to the judgment of his contemporaries that posterity appeals; and as men who knew the priceless worth of the deceased, not only in the high position which he held in our own State, but in all that exalts and adorns man's nature in the private walks of life, will Floridians lay their cypress boughs upon his tomb.

"The manifestation of a people's regard for the character and services of those luminaries whom death has removed from their counsels, but whose radiant brightness, still lighting the paths they tread, it cannot destroy, is at once an evidence of their gratitude to God and the highest incentive to imitate their worthy examples; for the noblest ambition of an exalted nature springs from the desire for a deathless name—of living in the estimation of the good in the dim and distant future. But for this pleasing hope, the spirits of earth's purest and best would sink beneath the cold neglect, the crushing toil, the base ingratitude for benefits conferred, which beset the path to fame.

"Universal as are the elements of greatness, governed as the Americans once were by the same laws and institutions, subject to similar social and political influences, and borne onward upon the same wave of development, there must necessarily be much in the history of distinguished Americans which is common to all. Bright constellations in the same great sphere, fixing the gaze and guiding the steps of their race, beaming with a '*firm, fixed and resting quality*,' while lesser orbs revolve and change around them, they but 'differ as one star differeth from another star in glory.'

"But affection's hand, recording the verdict of truth, will long with feeling trace that wealth of soul peculiarly his own, of Georgia's gifted son; and those who have heard his clarion voice, whose hearts have swelled under the outbursts of his impassioned soul, who in him have found a Roman firmness combined with all of woman's feeling and affection, will long recall that happy union of the noblest gifts of head and heart which stamped Howell Cobb with greatness.

"Throughout his long and arduous public career Mr. Cobb's hold upon the hearts and brains of the Southern people was its peculiar feature. Scorning disguise, surveying men and measures from the elevation of his own exalted nature, his public addresses, no less than his public and private conduct, inspired affection and commanded respect; and few public men have had more or truer friends.

"Empires and States have flourished and decayed, and shattered columns or buried tombs alone remain to tell their story; but in the providence of God, the memories of the noble intellects, the pure in heart, who have labored for the good of their race, and upon whose deeds His laws have stamped their approbation, live on for ever, not by, but above, the record of sculptured urn or monumental bust, in the proudest of all fanes—the hearts of the wise and just—and these constitute the noble few 'who were not born to die.'

"To this exalted fraternity will future generations assign the heroic Georgian; and though his grave be not upon his 'native heath,' it will still be sacred to all who love the brave and true, for

'Such graves are pilgrim shrines—
Shrines to no creed or code confined;
The Delphian vales, the Palestines,
The Meccas of the mind.'"

Even the pulpit did not neglect to signalize an event so universally lamented.

The following extract is from a sermon preached by Dr. William T. Brantly, of Atlanta, Georgia, shortly after Gov. Cobb's death. After elucidating the nature of that spiritual liberty which is the gift of "the Son" (John viii. 36), the Doctor labored to impress his congregation with the importance and wisdom of making *immediate* efforts to secure it. In this connection he said:

"The duty to which I have referred is impressively urged upon our consideration by that melancholy event which was yesterday announced to our community by a telegraphic despatch from New York. I allude to the death of the Hon. Howell Cobb. This occurrence, which has awakened sincere sorrow in many hearts all over our land, has covered with mourning the homes of several members of this church. An illustrious man has fallen. Whether we consider his intellectual endowments, the commanding force of his oratory, the extensive influence he wielded, the high positions he so long and so ably filled both in the State and the National councils, or his ardent and disinterested patriotism, it must be conceded by all parties that he was one of the most distinguished men Georgia has ever produced. Self-possessed, discriminating, prompt and impartial, he was, as a presiding officer, fully the peer of the ablest man who ever preceded or followed him in the Speaker's chair of the National House of Representatives. When Georgia passed her ordinance of secession, no man entered more earnestly and self-sacrificing than did he into the cause of Southern independence; and when that cause was overwhelmed with irretrievable disaster, no man was more truly afflicted.

"But the honors which men heaped upon him are of small value now.

> 'How loved, how valued once, avails thee not,
> To whom related, or by whom begot:
> A heap of dust alone remains of thee;
> 'Tis all thou art, and all the great shall be.'

"Was he a Christian? Had Christ invested

him with that exalted freedom of which I have been speaking to you this morning? He made no public profession of his faith in a divine Saviour; yet there is good reason for believing that the great question of his soul's salvation was with him a matter of profound concern, and that he was not a stranger to that preparation without which fallen man cannot meet his Maker in peace. Years ago, when I was his pastor in Athens, I had occasion to visit him during a period of domestic affliction, when, in answer to a question proposed, he said to me, 'I do not see how it is possible for any man to be without concern in regard to his spiritual condition.' Subsequently I met him at the bedside of his dying father. And when he saw how peacefully and even triumphantly his aged sire responded to the summons, from which, though a consistent Christian, he had recoiled through life, an impression was made on the mind of the son which was never effaced. Those who only saw him as he mingled among men in all the exuberance of his natural hilarity, had little idea of the spiritual strugglings which were progressing within.

"On one occasion, in his native town, he rose

before a large congregation and presented himself among those who were soliciting an interest in the prayers of Christian people. The last time I preached in the city of Macon (a few months ago) I saw him in the congregation, listening with reverent attention as I was attempting to present Jesus as the Way and the Life. Pious and judicious friends, to whom of late he more particularly disclosed his religious emotions, have told me since his death that he had given them very consoling evidence that he was a regenerated man. He signified to them and to others his determination to profess publicly his faith in Christ at an early day. There is ground, then, for believing that he was not a stranger to that faith which he did not openly avow, and that the blow which so instantaneously broke the 'pitcher at the fountain,' thus arresting with a mortal chill, the action of the natural heart, did not fall upon a heart spiritually unprepared for the solemn event. We may comfort ourselves with the persuasion that the summons which came 'like a clap of thunder in a cloudless sky' was but a call to 'depart and be with Christ, which is far better' than to be here.

"But let this startlingly sudden death admonish

us all. We must be insensible and stupid indeed if from this event we hear not a voice saying to us, 'Be ye also ready, for in such an hour as ye think not, the Son of Man cometh.' 'Whatsoever thy hand findeth to do, do it with thy might; for in the grave whither thou goest there is no work, nor knowledge, nor wisdom, nor device.'"

LAMENTATION.

But now he is dead, wherefore should I fast? Can I bring him back again? I shall go to him, but he shall not return to me.—2 Samuel xii. 23.

Weep not for the dead, neither bemoan him; but weep for him that goeth away; for he shall return no more, nor see his native country.—Jeremiah xxii. 10.

But I would not have you ignorant, brethren, concerning them which are asleep, that ye sorrow not, even as others which have no hope. For if we believe that Jesus died and rose again, even so them also which sleep in Jesus will God bring with him.—1 Thessalonians, iv. 13, 14.

For whom the Lord loveth he chasteneth, and scourgeth every son whom he receiveth.—Hebrews xii. 6.

The sorrows of my spirit are enlarged,
  My eyes are full of tears;
The grief with which my soul is overcharged
  Excites strange doubts and fears:
Alas! I seek, I call, in vain, in vain,
On earthly friendships to relieve my pain!

We grieve to think our eyes no more
  That form, those features loved, shall trace;
But sweet it is, from memory's store,
  To call each fondly cherished grace,
  And fold them in the heart's embrace.
No bliss 'mid worldly crowds is bred
Like musing on the sainted dead.

II.

LAMENTATION.

THE news of the death of Gen. Cobb reached Athens, Georgia, on the 9th of October. On Monday, the 12th, a meeting of the citizens was held at the Town Hall, for the purpose of expressing their deep sorrow at his death, and of testifying their respect and reverence for his memory.

The following are the official minutes of that meeting, with the exception of the addresses, which were furnished at the special request of the editor:

Public Meeting.

Monday, October 12, 1868.

The citizens of Athens met in solemn assembly at noon to-day, to pay the last public tribute to the memory of a great man, occasioned by the sudden, sorrowful and lamented death of our gifted Statesman, our noble Patriot, our generous Friend, our eloquent Orator, our sage Counselor and our brave Defender—Hon. Howell Cobb; James D. Pittard, Intendant, presiding, and Albert L. Mitchell, acting as Secretary.

The Chairman stated the object of the meeting as above recorded.

Gen. William M. Browne moved that a committee of seven be appointed to draft resolutions to be submitted to the meeting. The Chair appointed Gen. William M. Browne, Colonel Stevens Thomas, Major M. Stanley, Judge Y. L. G. Harris, John H. Newton, Hon. Junius Hillyer and Colonel B. C. Yancey, who reported the following resolutions through the Chairman, Gen. Browne, who in presenting them, eulogized the life and character of the deceased:

Speech of Gen. William M. Browne.

Mr. Chairman and Fellow-citizens: The duty devolves upon me, as Chairman of the committee which has been appointed to prepare resolutions on the mournful occasion which has called us together to-day, to report the result of our deliberations. In doing so, sir, I cannot refrain from saying that never, during the course of a not uneventful life, have I been required to discharge a duty which caused me profounder sorrow or severer pain.

Howell Cobb was the dearest and best friend I had on earth. I have known him well and intimately for many years. Our friendship was of the warmest, closest and most cordial character. I felt toward him the affection of a brother, I gave him the confidence of a brother, and it is among the most comforting of my reflections now, in my great grief, that he fully and warmly reciprocated that affection and that confidence. In all our association, during all the years of our companionship, there never was a moment when our friendship was interrupted by the slightest jar or misunderstanding. You all, gentlemen, have lost a valued friend. I have lost an only brother; for, had he been my brother by blood as well as by affection, I could not have loved him better. David did not love Jonathan more truly than I loved Howell Cobb.

He was one of the greatest and best men I have ever known. He was the most generous, tolerant, unselfish man I ever knew. He was the best husband, the most affectionate son, the most indulgent parent, the most steadfast friend, the most genial companion. I do not believe that an ungenerous or uncharitable wish ever found a resting-place in his great heart; and even toward the few who could be called his enemies, I know that he entertained no feelings of lasting animosity or ill will. On the contrary, I have known him put himself to trouble and inconvenience to serve and gratify men who had maligned his character and had attempted to sully his fame. Not long ago, conversing with me about a man with whom at one time he was upon friendly terms, but who had been for many years among the most unscrupulous and vindictive of his enemies, he remarked, in reply to some indignant observation of mine, "Notwithstanding all that ——— has done to forfeit my respect, there is a kind place in my heart for that man yet." And almost at the hour when his noble nature found expression in that sentiment of forgiveness, the man of whom he spoke was attempting to represent him as cruel, malevolent and uncharitable.

Here, in this presence, I feel that it would be

almost presumptuous for me to consider and discuss at any length the character and merits of my lamented friend. At another time that duty will, doubtless, be performed, and will be entrusted to abler hands than mine. But in the reverence paid to his memory, to his private worth and to those lovable qualities which made everybody who knew him his friend, we may participate now, with all propriety and earnestness of feeling. We have all known him in private life. We have seen him mingle in our social circles. We have known his mode and way of life, and many of you whom I see here to-day have known him from his boyhood up. We can testify to the perfect uprightness and purity of his character, the simplicity of his habits, the affability of his manners, the cheerfulness of his conversation and his unchanging fidelity to his friends. We can testify, too, to his great benevolence and his munificent charities dispensed, not ostentatiously or fitfully, but in secret and as the constant pleasure of his life, diffusing comfort and gladness around him. Oh, my friends, I could pour out my heart like water in speaking of the great virtues which were embodied in the character and exemplified by the conduct of our deceased friend—virtues which we all loved to contemplate with gratitude and admiration, which were a load-stone attracting to itself universal confidence, universal love and universal respect; and the recollection of which, descending with time, will be for ever cherished so long as the great and the good are objects of regard.

I confess, gentlemen, that I can scarcely realize the dreadful reality that I shall never see my friend again in life; that I shall never hear his cheerful voice, never listen to his affectionate counsel, never again grasp his honest hand. But it is so. He is gone—gone for ever. The place which knew him once so well will know him no more, and all that is left to you and to me is to drop a tear upon his grave and treasure his memory in our hearts so long as we live.

The following are the resolutions, alike exceedingly appropriate in character and felicitous in expression:

Whereas, In his inscrutable wisdom, it has pleased Almighty God to remove from among us, our beloved friend and esteemed fellow-citizen, Howell Cobb, whose childhood, early manhood and maturer years were spent in our midst, whose name and fame were objects of our pride, admiration and respect, and who was endeared to us by the strongest ties of intimate association; and,

Whereas, While we bow in humble submission to the will of Him who orders all things for good, and who has seen fit to visit our community with this heavy and unexpected calamity, as the friends, companions of his boyhood and manhood, and neighbors of the deceased, we would testify the heartfelt sorrow with which we mourn his loss, the profound respect which we feel for his eminent character, exalted virtues and commanding talents, and the affectionate remembrance in which we hold those many genial social qualities which made his friendship so dear, and his society so charming; and,

Whereas, It is the duty of every Georgian to record his respect for the memory of one whose life of eminent public service in all the high and responsible offices which he filled, was spent in ceaseless effort to promote the welfare and uphold the honor and dignity of Georgia, it is especially proper for us who knew and loved him best, in addition to a recognition of his public service, to render to his generous, unselfish character and private worth, ere the portals of the tomb close over him for ever, every tribute of regard, respect and reverence of which our hearts are capable; Therefore be it

Resolved, As the sense of the citizens of Athens that in the death of Gen. Howell Cobb, we have each lost a valued friend, our town a high-minded and honored citizen, our State a noble, gifted and devoted Son, and our country a true Patriot and a great Statesman.

Resolved, That the citizens of Athens will attend the funeral in a body, and that the Faculty and Students of the University and the High School, the members of the two Literary Societies, the Masonic Fraternity and the Society of Odd Fellows, and the Fire Companies be invited to participate with us in the discharge of this mournful duty.

Resolved, That the Chair be requested to appoint one hundred citizens as a special guard of honor to meet the remains on their arrival, and escort them from the depôt.

Resolved, That a Committee of three be appointed by the Chair to communicate the foregoing to the afflicted widow and the family of the deceased, and to offer to her and to them the most heartfelt expression of our deep sympathy and respect.

Resolved, That the proceedings of this meeting be published in the town papers.

William M. Browne,
Stevens Thomas,
M. Stanley,
Y. L. G. Harris,
John H. Newton,
Junius Hillyer,
Benjamin C. Yancey.

The resolutions were unanimously adopted; after which Hon. Junius Hillyer eloquently spoke of the virtue, integrity, nobility and grandeur of the character of Gen. Cobb from his infancy to his grave.

Address of Hon. Junius Hillyer.

Mr. Chairman: Forty-eight years ago I saw Gen. Cobb for the first time. He was standing in the middle of the street between the post-office corner and the Lombard building. He was five years old, and I was thirteen.

Being surprised to see so small a boy alone in the street, I asked him who he was. He told me his name was Howell Cobb.

From that time to the close of his life I knew him. He was a sprightly, remarkable boy, and attracted much attention. Everybody in town knew of him and spoke of him. From his boyhood through his whole life, his cheerful, genial temper rendered his society peculiarly attractive. When he was admitted to the Bar, he was for a short time associated with me in the practice of law. In 1837 he was elected by the Legislature, Solicitor of the Western Circuit, and for three years he filled that office with distinguished ability, and was, indeed, a terror to evil-doers. In 1842 he was selected by a Convention of the Democratic party as one of its candidates for Congress, and was in the same year elected. Notwithstanding his youth, he took a high position in Congress among the leaders of his party, and early distinguished himself as one of the statesmen of the country.

In his political life, Gen. Cobb rose far above the position of a mere party leader.

His statesmanship reached a high nationality, and embraced within its comprehension all the interests of his country. Throughout the whole breadth of the realm, the views of Gen. Cobb were understood and quoted as authority; and in all the civilized nations of the world, whenever the affairs and policy of America were spoken of, the name of Howell Cobb was known, and his position on the various questions of public interest was commented on, as having great weight with the American people and entitled to the greatest respect abroad. He was eminently a national man, and his reputation constitutes a part of the rich treasure of the American people. In 1849 he was chosen Speaker of the House of Representatives, and in that position he added new fame to his exalted character, manifesting an administrative ability that greatly distinguished him. In 1851 he was elected Governor of the State of Georgia, when he greatly advanced the interests of the State. In 1855 he was again elected to Congress. In 1857 he was chosen a member of Mr. Buchanan's Cabinet and placed at the head of the Treasury Department. Upon his recommendation and at his request I was selected as the law officer of the Treasury Department, which placed me near his person and brought me in close connection with a very large portion of his official duties, and enables me to speak from my own knowledge of the wisdom and integrity of his administration. All the bonds given by the principal officers of the Government, and all contracts with the department passed under my supervision. All suits brought by the Government for debts, except in the Post-office Department, were under my control, and all claims upon the Treasury were submitted to me for my opinion. I mention this to show how intimate and extensive was my connection with Gen. Cobb in the discharge of our official duties, and how I had opportunity to observe and to know his honesty and integrity and his great administrative power. I can speak here from my own knowledge. My frequent long, careful and confidential consultations with him and his faithful Assistant Secretary, Mr. Clayton, enable me to speak of his wisdom, his careful, conscientious regard for the law and the true interests of the Treasury.

Toward the close of Mr. Buchanan's administration, Gen. Cobb left the Cabinet and returned to Georgia, to take part in the great movement that then convulsed the State. He believed that the ascendency of the abolition sentiment in the Government of the United States prostrated all hope that the property and interests of the Southern

States would be protected by that Government, and he believed that the only safety for the South was in a withdrawal from the Union. He was a member of the Convention that adopted the Confederate Constitution, and was also a member of the Provisional Congress at Montgomery, Alabama. Early in the war he raised a regiment with the rank of Colonel, and was soon promoted to be Brigadier-General, and was again promoted to be Major-General, which position he held in the Confederate army at the time of the surrender. After the surrender he was arrested at his house in this town by United States soldiers and ordered to Washington. On the way he was stopped by orders from President Johnson, and discharged from arrest, as was supposed at the instance of Gen. Grant.

Thus I have rapidly and briefly sketched the public life of Gen. Cobb from its commencement to its close. I know I have not done it justice. I have not attempted that. It will be left for him who writes the history of the American Government for the last twenty-five years to do justice to the name and character of Gen. Cobb. I must only stand here among you, his neighbors and lifelong friends, to briefly tell you what you all know. No man knew Gen. Cobb better than I did. For thirty years we were engaged in the practice of law in the same courts. We have traveled thousands of miles in the same buggy. For more than twenty years we often occupied the same room at the hotels. I have often been opposed to him and associated with him in the trial of the most important causes involving the life, liberty and property of our clients. When opposed to Gen. Cobb, I well knew that I had nothing to hope from any oversight or mistake. I well knew that every point of law would be taken and every point in the testimony would be presented and commented on. But it was when associated with him in the trial of important causes that I had an opportunity of observing the strength and breadth of his intellect. Often we have been engaged till a late hour of the night in consultation on some case then being on trial or soon to be called. It was there, around the consultation-table, that Gen. Cobb should have been seen to be fully appreciated. There were exhibited his cool sagacity and his careful, unwearied attention to all the points of law and fact. It was there that his associate counsel felt the strength that he brought to the cause, and learned to lean on him with hope and confidence.

I have referred to Gen. Cobb's genial and attractive temper. But it was on the circuit that his social qualities rose to absolute splendor. It was on the circuit that everybody gathered around him to enjoy his company. Those who never traveled the Western Circuit can never fully know how pleasant a man he was.

But Gen. Cobb is gone and the Bar of the Western Circuit is gone. Mr. Paine, Gen. Harden, Judge Harris, Judge Dougherty, Judge Dawson, Judge Cone, Judge Lumpkin, Col. Stanford, Mr. J. Peeples, Mr. Overby, Mr. Haygood, Col. Deloney, Capt. Temple Cooper, Mr. R. Milligan, Col. Wm. Milligan, Col. McMillan, Mr. Malcome, J. Walker and Gen. Thos. R. R. Cobb are all dead. Col. Foster, Mr. C. Peeples, Judge Jackson, Mr. Hull and Judge Underwood have left the circuit. Two or three old men still linger and look back and remember scenes and places that we no longer visit. And now the bright star of the Western Circuit has gone down for ever, and a great light is this day extinguished. How sad are these reflections and how sad is this crowning hour! Melancholy yet pleasant is the memory of days long—*long* ago, when my lamented friend would often take me home with him, and with his then young and beautiful bride extend to me a genial hospitality. I ever felt welcome at his board and with his family. Surely it becomes me to speak at his funeral and to mingle my tears with those who mourn for him.

And now, my young friends, in view of this solemn occasion, and of these sad reminiscences, may I not say a word to you—a word of warning and of counsel? It has been said of Gen. Cobb that a great man has this day fallen in Israel; it may also be said a strong man has fallen. He was remarkable for his powers of endurance and for the strength of his constitution. I have known him to endure for many hours the extreme severity of cold and heat, of storms of snow and rain, and yet I never heard him complain of cold or fatigue. And yet, my young friends, he is gone. His strength, his endurance and the soundness of his constitution could not save him. Let his sudden, premature death be a warning to you and to us all. Gen. Cobb never united himself with any ecclesiastical organization. But I have reason to know that religion had made a deep impression on his mind, and that from his heart went up with fervent emotion many an earnest prayer that the world knew not of.

Young gentlemen, I can commend to you the example of Gen. Cobb in his social and political life, and I will venture also to commend his religious emotions.

My friends, let us be warned by the sudden departure of our friend to remember how frail we are, and to prepare to obey when we are called, and to unite with him and with one another in that mansion in the heavens, eternal, not made with hands, prepared by our Saviour for his people.

Remarks of Hon. Benj. C. Yancey.

Athens, Ga., April 22, 1869.

Rev. S. Boykin, *Macon:*

My Dear Sir: You solicit a copy of remarks made by me, in October last, before an assemblage of citizens of this place, on the occasion of the sad news of the sudden death, in New York City, of our distinguished citizen—Hon. Howell Cobb.

You desire it for publication in a Book Memorial of the illustrious dead.

I have hesitated to comply with your wish, from a consciousness of my inability to reproduce the words extemporized—the inspiration of sensibilities deeply moved by the unexpected and sudden dispensation of Providence.

But my love for the dead, a sense of duty to contribute my mite to cherish his memory, and a hope that the contribution of my testimony to your Memorial may result in aiding to win young men to practice the virtues of the lamented Cobb, constrain me to yield to your request.

I furnish a condensed statement of my line of thought as well as I can recall the expression:

The resolutions in honor of Gov. Cobb meet my approval. It had been my privilege to enjoy his friendship and confidence for thirty-five years. Memory traced its manifestations through a period of more than a third of a century to an acquaintance formed in college life. In the halls of the university in this town a friendship was formed which lapse of years, distance of residence, and occasional differences of political opinion and conduct, never weakened. He was two years my senior, and at that period in advance of me in college classes; but there was more intimacy between us than is usual between senior and sophomore. We were in the same literary society, and after graduation, being a resident of Athens, he studied law here and continued frequently to attend and participate in the weekly debates in the Phi-Kappa Society. Through that period of three years and more of personal intercourse, he manifested that ardent, unselfish affection, generous, magnanimous impulses of the heart, quickness and vigor of mind, all of which he developed and displayed in greater maturity and power in the numerous official positions, State and Federal, to which he was called in subsequent life.

Very few men have ever possessed his vivacity of spirit, his social nature, his popularity of address, winning the esteem of all classes of Society—low and high, poor and rich, ignorant and learned. It was a magnetic power, originating from a heart full, generous, enlarged—embracing humanity. His rapid bound, in very early manhood into Congress, and subsequent rapid promotion to various high official positions, were not, therefore, matters of surprise. He was a man endowed with rare gifts. To these he united an unusually accurate knowlege of human nature and great sagacity as a statesman.

Though our pathways in life till a few years

back had been in different States, yet his public positions brought him under my observation, and my domestic associations in this town of his residence often placed us in maturer life in personal intercourse. For a few years we had been fellow-citizens here. My opportunities, therefore, for knowing the man had been full.

I would not undertake to elaborate upon the enlarged official life of the lamented Cobb. He had been Solicitor-general of this Judicial Circuit; had served several terms in the House of Representatives of the Congress of the United States, in which he had been speaker; filled the gubernatorial office of the State; was Secretary of the Treasury—a member of the Cabinet of President Buchanan; was President of the Provisional Congress of the Confederate Government; Colonel and General in the Confederate Army; had been my associate in the Board of Trustees of the University of the State. Suffice it to say, that he filled every position with ability and honor; and throughout life, whenever opportunity was presented, displayed the benevolence of his great heart.

He is gone! Called hence by his Creator, in the full maturity of his intellect and manhood, with but a moment's warning. We should derive from this sudden and inscrutable dispensation of Providence the instruction that in the midst of life we are in death, and heed the voice of *Wisdom:* "Therefore, be ye also ready; for in such an hour as ye think not the Son of man cometh." "For as the lightning cometh out of the east, and shineth even unto the west, so shall the coming of the Son of man be."

Each one of us might be profited by studying the character and practicing the virtues of our lamented, distinguished citizen. We should cherish the memory of *Howell Cobb.*

Respectfully,

BENJAMIN C. YANCEY.

Mr. Yancey, on taking his seat, was followed by Col. Stevens Thomas, who, in melancholy beauty, portrayed the sincerity, the nobility, the grandeur and the sublimity of Gen. Cobb's true manhood.

[The editor regrets that he is not able to furnish an exact copy of Col. Stevens Thomas' address. The accompanying letter shows that the substance only of the speech is given.]

ATHENS, GA., NOV. 21, 1868.

REV. SAMUEL BOYKIN, *Macon, Ga.:*

DEAR SIR: Your favor of the 8th instant was duly received, and I avail myself of the first leisure moment to reply.

I have endeavored to write out (recalling as well I could the precise language) the *substance* of the remarks made by me at the meeting of citizens of this place on the occasion of the death of Gen. Cobb, and herewith enclose a copy of the same.

Very respectfully yours, etc.,

S. THOMAS.

REMARKS OF COL. STEVENS THOMAS.

MR. CHAIRMAN: I might leave to others and the quiet reflections of my own mind a review of the life and character of our illustrious friend and fellow-citizen. But a grateful recollection of his confidence and friendship impels me to unite my humble voice with that of others in this sad requiem to his memory. The voice now hushed in death ever spoke to me the words of kindness and sympathy, and language would fail me in the attempt to express the emotions which I felt upon the startling announcement of his sudden and untimely fall.

Sir, it was my privilege to know Gen. Cobb long and well, and I can, with all truthfulness, say that I never knew in him an instance of a departure from the standard of a refined and lofty sense of honor. Besides that remarkable magnanimity of character which he so often exhibited, and which has been so appropriately alluded to by others on this occasion, there was another characteristic, to my mind equally rare and striking — it was his unaffected simplicity of character. No man was freer from vanity or conventionalism; whether in prosperity or adversity, in private life or in high public position, he was ever the same, unchanged by circumstance or condition; and he won all hearts which came within the magic circle of his influence, no less by the charms of his intellect than by the genial warmth of his frank, manly nature.

In the private and intimate relations which he sustained to his kindred and his friends, it is but simple truth to say that he was all the tenderest affection could claim or the warmest friendship demand.

Of his long, successful public career this is not the proper occasion to speak, but I may say that he truly filled the measure of a patriot's duty; for his entire mature life was devoted to the service of his country.

With firm and unfaltering step he trod the difficult paths that lead to political preferment. As he advanced from one commanding position to another, it seemed to those of us who started with him in the race of life as if his vision grew and expanded with the horizon to which he attained. Identified as he was, to a large extent, with many of the great events of the time in which he lived, both before and during the late war, he proved himself equal to any emergency, and sustained himself with marked ability among men whose renown is imperishable.

But he is gone! Stricken in the full maturity of vigorous manhood, like some majestic oak towering above the surrounding forest, he has suddenly fallen, and the reverberations of his fall, resounding far and near, touch a responsive chord in every sympathetic heart; and though that manly form is now clothed in the habiliments of the grave, and that eye, which so beamed with light and every generous emotion, is now closed in the night of death, yet will the memory of his eminent public worth and generous nature live long after most of us, who pay this unavailing tribute to his memory, shall have passed to that spirit-land to which he has but preceded us by a few short, fleeting years.

The following gentlemen were appointed a Committee of Condolence to extend to the grief-stricken family the heartfelt sympathies of this whole community. Committee—Gen. Wm. M. Browne, Col. Stevens Thomas, Mr. John H. Newton,

A committee, consisting of Dr. R. M. Smith, Judge Y. L. G. Harris, Hon. Junius Hillyer, Col. Benjamin C. Yancey, Maj. M. Stanley, E. P. Lumpkin, Esq., and Mr. L. J. Lampkin, was appointed to co-operate with the family of the deceased in making arrangements for the funeral.

In obedience to the resolutions, one hundred citizens were appointed as a special guard of honor to meet the remains on their arrival, and escort them from the depôt.

Capt. H. A. Gartrell, Dr. E. D. Newton, Capt. Frank Pope, Dr. William King, Dr. H. R. J. Long, Capt. Richard J. Wilson, Mr. W. G. Noble, and W. W. Lumpkin, Esq., were appointed a committee of citizens to join with the committee from the City Council, and meet the body at Union Point and attend it to Athens.

Upon motion of Capt. H. A. Gartrell, the Committee of Arrangements, consisting of Dr. R. M. Smith, Col. Benjamin C. Yancey and others, were instructed to select some suitable person to deliver an eulogy upon the life and character of General HOWELL COBB, and that said committee confer with a committee appointed by the Phi-Kappa Society for a similar purpose.

Upon motion the meeting adjourned.

JAMES D. PITTARD, Intendant, Chairman.

ALBERT L. MITCHELL, Secretary.

COUNCIL CHAMBER.

ATHENS, October 12, 1868.

The Board of Wardens was called together this morning to take suitable action upon the melancholy occurrence of the death of our esteemed and distinguished fellow-citizen, Hon. HOWELL COBB, who hath so recently and so suddenly passed away. His Honor, Intendant Pittard, presided. Wardens Thomas, Ritch, Billups, Lumpkin, Dobbs and Beusse were present, being a full meeting of the Board.

Warden Billups moved that a committee of three be appointed to draft resolutions expressive of the regret, the sorrow and the grief of Athens at the loss of so great and so noble a man.

The committee appointed were Wardens Billups, Thomas and Lumpkin, who reported the following resolutions, which were unanimously adopted:

Preamble and Resolutions.—A great man has fallen. Gen. Howell Cobb, a resident of Athens for much the larger part of his life, will be seen in our midst no more. Suddenly, on the morning of the 9th instant, in the city of New York, "the silver cord was loosed," and his noble spirit passed from earth. Alas! for the country that such a loss should come upon it at such a time! An incorruptible patriot, a wise statesman, an accomplished orator, a gallant soldier, a generous man and an unfaltering friend, his death will be deplored by the wise and the good, by the brave and the true-hearted everywhere.

But by us, as Georgians, and especially as citizens of Athens, among whom he lived so long, and by whom he was so much loved and honored, this most sad event cannot but be regarded with peculiar grief and poignancy.

Therefore be it resolved,

1. That, in humble submission to Almighty God, we mourn the death of Gen. Howell Cobb with a sorrow the most sincere and profound.

2. That by his fidelity and ability in all the high positions which he filled; and by his noble and generous bearing as a citizen, and in all the relations of life, he has left a name which we will proudly cherish and hand down in honor to posterity.

3. That we tender to the bereaved family of the deceased our deepest and most unfeigned sympathy, and our earnest hopes that in their great affliction they may be sustained by the hand of Him who loves while he chastens.

4. That the Intendant be instructed to appoint a committee of the Council to meet the remains at Union Point and attend them to Athens.

5. That the Intendant be requested to appoint a committee of seven citizens to act conjointly with the family of the deceased in making arrangements for the funeral.

6. That this preamble and these resolutions be placed among the records of the Council, and published with the proceedings, and that a copy, signed in due form, be transmitted to the bereaved family.

H. C. Billups, Chairman.
J. J. Thomas,
Frank Lumpkin.

In conformity to the fourth resolution, a committee, consisting of Wardens Ritch, Beusse, Lumpkin and Thomas, was appointed to meet the remains at Union Point and attend them to Athens.

Upon motion, the Board adjourned.

A. L. MITCHELL, Clerk of Council.

The PHI-KAPPA SOCIETY, of which Gov. Cobb was an honorary member, also evinced its high respect for the deceased by adopting the following preamble and resolutions:

UNIVERSITY OF GEORGIA.

PHI-KAPPA HALL, October 12, 1868.

"The Reaper, whose name is Death," has come again with his scythe and removed from our midst the most venerated, respected and beloved of our honorary brothers. When least expected he came to do his solemn and terrible work. At no time is he welcome, but when he comes to bear away in the evening of life the man of a well-spent and glorious career, the sadness of his advent is alleviated by the mellowing glow of the illustrious example left to posterity.

Death has been in the literary circle of our brotherhood, and borne from us the noblest of the noble, the wisest of the wise and the truest of the true. Gen. HOWELL COBB "sleeps the sleep that knows no waking." Realizing the irreparable loss we have sustained, in common with our whole country, we as a body would express our profound respect for his memory, and our deep sympathy for his large and affectionate family, in this the sad hour of their bereavement. Whether we contemplate the deceased as a friend, a patriot, a soldier or a statesman, we find him ever the same generous, noble, prompt, brave, enthusiastic spirit, who, knowing the truth and the right, dared both to maintain. We breathe the universal sentiment of all classes, the poor and the rich, the ignorant and the learned, the false and the true, when we say a great man has fallen—the protector of the oppressed and the friend of the poor. Humbly submitting to the divine edict of the King of kings and Lord of lords in removing from us our honorary brother, we, the Phi-Kappa Society, *do resolve:*

1. That in the death of Gen. Howell Cobb our society has lost one of her oldest and most respected members, our State her noblest son, who, identified more with her past history than any one within her borders, has ever sustained in the high-

est offices of her gift the same unswerving integrity and faithful adherence to her social and political interests; the poor their best friend, education her warmest advocate, and those connected to him by the nearest and dearest relations of life, a heart whose nobleness, kindness and unselfish affection they alone can fully appreciate.

2. That we tender to his grief-stricken family the assurances of our heartfelt sympathy in this the season of their sad affliction.

3. That the members of this society attend in a body the remains of our deceased brother to the grave, and that we wear the usual badge of mourning for the space of thirty days in honor of his memory.

4. That a copy of this preamble and these resolutions be furnished the family of the deceased, that the same be published in the city papers, and their publication earnestly requested by the press of the State.

John E. Donalson, Chairman.
N. E. Harris,
John D. Rambo.

The body of Gov. Cobb, suitably escorted, reached

Savannah by steamer on the 14th of October, and was conveyed immediately to Athens, Georgia, by a special train. The escort on its way to Athens was swelled by the addition of delegations, personal friends and admirers, who from all parts of the State were wending their way to the city of Athens to pay the last funeral honors to the lamented dead.

The solemn tolling of the college bell announced to all, about the dawn of day on the morning of the 15th, that the remains had arrived.

THE GRAVE.

Whatsoever thy hand findeth to do, do it with thy might; for there is no work, nor device, nor knowledge, nor wisdom in the grave, whither thou goest.—Ecclesiastes ix. 10.

The Lord killeth and maketh alive; he bringeth down to the grave, and bringeth up.—1 Samuel ii. 6.

God will redeem my soul from the power of the grave; for he shall receive me.—Psalm xlix. 15.

I will ransom them from the power of the grave; I will redeem them from death: O death, I will be thy plagues: O grave, I will be thy destruction.—Hosea xiii. 14.

Hail, heavenly voice, once heard in Patmos! "Write,
  Henceforth the dead who die in Christ are blest:
  Yea, saith the Spirit, for they now shall rest
From all their labors!" But no dull, dark night
That rest o'ershadows: 'tis the dayspring bright
  Of bliss; the foretaste of a richer feast;
  A sleep, if sleep it be, of lively zest,
Peopled with visions of intense delight.
And though the secrets of that resting-place
  The soul embodied knows not; yet she knows
No sin is there, God's likeness to deface,
  To stint his love—no purgatorial woes;
Her dross is left behind, nor mixture base
  Mars the pure stream of the serene repose.

'Tis a blessing to live, but a greater to die,
And the best of the world is its path to the sky.
Be it gloomy or bright, for the life that he gave
Let us thank him—but blessed be God for the grave!
'Tis the end of our toil, 'tis the crown of our bliss,
'Tis the portal of happiness—ay, but for this,
How hopeless were sorrow, how narrow were love,
If they looked not from earth to the rapture above!

III.

THE GRAVE.

A COMMITTEE of one hundred citizens received the corpse and bore it in solemn silence into the city, where they were joined by the citizens generally, who, amid tears and lamentations, united in escorting the body to the Town Hall. There it was deposited in state, and permitted to remain until three o'clock, attended by a guard of honor. During the day hundreds came to gaze for the last time upon the coffin of one they had so long loved and revered. The coffin itself was placed upon a stand covered with black velvet, and the hall was hung with mourning drapery. The coffin remained unopened, and the sorrowing visitors were only enabled, with saddened hearts and moistened eyes, to read the following inscription:

Gov. Howell Cobb,
Died October 9, 1868,
Aged 55 years and one month;

then, with saddened countenance, they would turn and depart, without uttering a word.

At three o'clock the following distinguished gentlemen, with crape upon their hats, and long white sashes across their shoulders, bore the coffin forth and placed it in a handsome hearse, drawn by four splendid horses: Col. Billups, Stevens Thomas, Judge Hillyer, Young L. G. Harris, Ferdinand Phinizy, F. W. Adams, Gen. William M. Browne, Col. D. C. Barrow.

Then the procession was formed in the following order:

1. Ministers of the Gospel.
2. Order of Free Masons.
3. Hearse, attended by Pall-bearers.
4. Family and Relations of the deceased.
5. Members of the Bar.
6. Trustees and Faculty of the University.
7. Literary Societies of the University.
8. Teachers and Pupils of the University High School.
9. Independent Order of Odd Fellows.

10. Intendant and Wardens of Athens, and other city and town officials.

11. Special Committees representing other communities.

12. Representatives of the Press.

13. Citizens on foot.

14. Citizens in Carriages and on Horseback.

With slow and solemn steps the procession wound through the streets and entered the college chapel, speedily filling the large building. Ministers of the Gospel and members of the Bar from all parts of the State occupied the platform, in front of which, and covered with garlands of flowers, was placed the costly coffin, upon an elevated stand festooned gracefully with evergreen wreaths. The entire chapel, draped in mourning by loving hands, wore a most funereal aspect, and a sensation of irrepressible sadness and solemnity pervaded the vast assembly. Low sobbing was heard, and tears of grief coursed down many cheeks. The order and character of the exercises in the chapel accorded with the solemnity of the occasion, and with the dignity of the personage whom they were intended to honor.

First, a solemn requiem was sung by the choir,

and then Rev. R. K. Porter, Pastor of the Presbyterian Church in Atlanta, Georgia, read the following selections from the Scriptures:

"We are strangers before thee, and sojourners, as were all our fathers: our days on the earth are as a shadow, and there is none abiding. Lord, make me to know mine end, and the measure of my days, what it is, that I may know how frail I am. For I know that thou wilt bring me to death, and to the house appointed for all living. Then shall the dust return to the earth as it was, and the spirit shall return unto God who gave it. If a man die, shall he live again?

"Jesus said unto her (Martha), I am the resurrection and the life. He that believeth in me, though he were dead, yet shall he live: and whosoever liveth and believeth in me, shall never die. I know that my Redeemer liveth, and that he shall stand at the latter day, upon the earth: and though after my skin worms destroy this body, yet in my flesh shall I see God; whom I shall see for myself, and mine eyes shall behold, and not another. My flesh also shall rest in hope; for thou wilt not leave my soul in hell; neither wilt thou suffer thine holy one to see corruption. Knowing that He which raised up the Lord Jesus, shall raise up us also by Jesus, and shall present us with you.

"I would not have you to be ignorant, brethren, concerning them which are asleep, that ye sorrow not, even as others which have no hope. For if we believe that Jesus died, and rose again, even so them also which sleep in Jesus will God bring with him. Wherefore comfort one another with these words. For I reckon that the sufferings of this present time are not worthy to be compared with the glory which shall be revealed in us. For the earnest expectation of the creature waiteth for the manifestation of the sons of God. For the creature was made subject to vanity, not willingly, but by reason of Him who hath subjected the same in hope: because the creature shall be delivered from the bondage of corruption unto the glorious liberty of the children of God. And we ourselves groan within ourselves, waiting for the adoption—to wit, the redemption of our body. For we know that if our earthly house of this tabernacle were dissolved, we have a building of God, a house not made with hands, eternal in the heavens. For in this we groan, earnestly desiring to be clothed upon with our house which is from heaven, if so be that being clothed we shall not be found naked. For we that are in this tabernacle do groan, being burdened, not for that we would be unclothed, but clothed upon, that mortality might be swallowed up of life.

"Blessed and holy is he that hath part in the first resurrection: on such the second death hath no power, but they shall be priests of God and of Christ, and shall reign with him a thousand years."

Rev. P. H. Mell, D. D., Vice-Chancellor of the Georgia State University, then offered a short and fervent prayer, after which, Rev. J. D. Burkhead, Pastor of the Athens Presbyterian Church, read the following hymn, which the choir sang with great feeling:

Burial of a Christian Brother.

Brother, rest from sin and sorrow;
Death is o'er, and life is won;
On thy slumber dawns no morrow:
Rest; thine earthly race is run.

Brother, wake; the night is waning;
Endless day is round thee poured;
Enter thou the rest remaining
For the people of the Lord.

Brother, wake; for He who loved thee—
He who died that thou mightst live—
He who graciously approved thee—
Waits thy crown of joy to give.

Fare thee well; though woe is blending
With the tones of earthly love,
Triumph high and joy unending
Wait thee in the realms above.

At the conclusion of the hymn, Rev. E. W. Warren, Pastor of the First Baptist Church of Macon, Georgia, from the text, "Know ye not that a prince and a great man has fallen this day in Israel?" (2 Samuel iii. 28), preached the following

Funeral Discourse.

I do not rise before you to eulogize the honored dead. This is not the occasion, nor am I the man, to enter this inviting field of thought, or avail myself of so happy a subject. His eulogy is already in the hearts of the people.

As a citizen of Macon, I but represent the feelings of our city, and the sentiments of the committees here present, when I say we have come to mingle our tears with yours, and to make our sorrows one, and to claim the right of sharing with you in the melancholy privilege of paying the last tribute of affectionate regard to the dead, whose loss we mourn with unaffected grief—a loss to our city, to our State, to our country.

As his pastor, I came to bury, not to praise, my honored friend. Were I to utter a word of adulation, and that silent tongue could speak, it would say, "Forbear! only my life shall speak!" And so it shall be.

True greatness is manifested in that completeness of character which, with unusual force and faithfulness, meets the emergencies and performs the obligations of life. It rises with the occasion, let that be what it may, and acts well its part.

Passing over the political career of Gov. Cobb, which was characterized by special ability and commanding success; let us consider those elements of character which so much endeared him to us.

In his professional and social life he involuntarily attached to himself all who knew him. His warm heart and transparent nature, his frank and genial deportment, his courtesy and nobility of character, gave him a welcome at all times to our homes and to our hearts. The better he was known, the more he was appreciated: the nearer he was, the greater you perceived him to be. His attachments were unostentatious, natural, sincere. You were fully conscious that you enjoyed his friendship.

He had a just appreciation of the great brotherhood of man, and a heart that beat in unison with his race. He could weep with those that wept, and it was his pleasure to rejoice with those who rejoiced. If he could have wielded the sword of unlimited power, it would have been against the enemies of man. Could he have calmed the elements of discord, he would have said "Peace be still" to every passion in the heart of man that rises against his brother, and he would have fostered "peace on earth and good-will among men." Let not the tongue of political detraction rob his fair name of this good impulse of his noble heart. Personal wrongs he labored to forget; personal kindness shown to him was gratefully cherished. He possessed the charity which "rejoices not in iniquity, but rejoices in the truth." His aversion to whatever he considered unmanly and hypocritical amounted almost to intolerance, but to the common weaknesses and foibles of men he exercised the charity which "beareth all things, believeth all things, hopeth all things, endureth all things."

If his enemy were fallen and helpless, he was the first to reach forth his hand to raise him up. While his independent nature would never ask favors from an enemy, his magnanimous soul was ever ready to grant them.

"Give to him that asketh, and from him that would borrow turn not thou away." He felt the force of this precept in its fullest and most unrestricted sense. It was a law, the literal fulfillment of which was essential to the obligations of the common brotherhood of the race. The highest social well-being of man could not be secured without it. He lightened his own burdens by bearing those of others. The relief he afforded to the needy reflected its happy influence upon his own mind, and thus the enlarged benevolence of his nature contributed to that uniformly cheerful spirit which was so characteristic of the man.

In his law-office in Macon he kept his fund for the poor in a drawer always near him. When asked by the indigent for help, he always responded. He did not say, "Depart in peace, be ye warmed and filled," without giving them those things which were needful for the body, as too many do. His tender sympathy for the sufferings of others would have given him no rest if he had thus violated a vital law of its being. A single incident which I heard related of him will illustrate this excellent trait in his character. While a member of Congress in Washington, he was standing in the street one day conversing with another Representative, when a poor little girl presented herself and asked for money to buy bread and medicines for her sick mother. Gov. Cobb said to his companion, "We have but little to do this morning; let us accompany this child to her mother's home and see what her necessities are." Following her, they passed from street to street and from lane to lane, till they were beyond the city limits, and coming to a poor hovel on the common, they entered; and there on a threadbare couch lay a woman, the impersonation of poverty, want and suffering. He emptied his purse of its last dollar, and left the woman amazed at the unparalleled generosity of the stranger.

It is not surprising that he should have given her his last dollar when he witnessed her sufferings, but that he had a heart whose generosity prompted him to go so far, to follow a poor little girl through so many by-ways, to see and relieve a stranger of whom he had never before heard, and of whom it was not probable he would ever hear again, were very unusual acts in a prominent politician. How very few do we find who are so deeply interested in relieving the poor!—whose hearts are so deeply touched by the cry of a stranger! and who always gave freely and willingly to relieve their necessities! Too many seek excuses for not giving: he was always glad of an opportunity to bestow his bounty on a needy object.

"He that giveth to the poor lendeth to the Lord." Let us be careful not to confound this excellent virtue with religion, or to substitute the bestowment of alms for saving faith in the Mediator. Philanthropy is susceptible of very high development. It may be so refined that its sensitive nature is pained by the wants of others, so that it makes common cause with all known cases of suffering. One thus becomes, in all the better feelings of his nature, the brother of his race, and is in sympathy with the great heart of frail humanity; so that he is never happier than when "it goes well" with all around him; and in laboring to produce this good result he promotes his own peace of mind.

His domestic character was almost peerless. I will not enter the sacred precincts of the home-sanctuary, and there show you the revered husband and the honored father, but will speak a few words as to the character of that love which he bore to his children. It was greater than natural, and only less than Christian love. Too many parents seem to love their children only for time. Their parental love satisfies itself with supplying the wants of the present life, but forgets the soul's relations to the life to come. They exhaust their resources on worldly accomplishments exclusively, and without reference to their effects upon religious character. They are trained for society, and taught with care the graces of mannerism and the policies of worldly success, without giving special heed to the higher *principles* which constitute character, and without inculcating motives which impart virtue to noble actions.

Our friend could not give to his children religious training, for he did not profess to be religious; this duty in its positive enforcement was left to her whose uniform example constantly said to them,

"This is the way—walk ye in it." But he carefully withheld every thought and word which in his opinion would discourage or hinder the Christian mother in this pious work. It was one of the troubles of his life that he could not with his views conscientiously lead the way for his children. He has been heard to say with tears that it would be his greatest happiness if he could, by becoming fully identified with the Church, give his unqualified endorsement of religion to his family. This unusual display of *pious* affection by one who did not profess to be a Christian himself, is only to be explained by the deep moral lessons which were imparted to him in tender years, and which had grown with his growth and strengthened with his strength. These early impressions had produced in his own bosom struggles for a personal interest in the truths of Christianity, which became a source of perpetual anxiety to him.

The greatest men are deficient without the gifts and graces imparted by the religion of Jesus Christ, the Mediator between God and man. The most excellent moral characters are wanting if this be absent. Without it, jealousy made Saul a murderer; ambition made Bonaparte a heartless despoiler of nations; and vanity dwarfed Voltaire into contemptible littleness. But with it, Luther, the obscure monk, shook the Vatican to its centre, and filled the world with hope of release from spiritual vassalage and superstition. He rose to the most exalted heights of moral heroism, and left free to the gaze of an anxious world the open pages of the hitherto sealed Book. With it, Daniel, for a time, dissipated the dark gloom that had so long rested, as a pall of moral night upon the Babylonish empire.

Without it, how sadly incomplete would be the character of our honored friend!—how deeply melancholy would be this occasion! But now a light springs up and the darkness disappears.

As his pastor, I claim the privilege of stating some facts as to the religious character of Gov. Cobb.

The obstacle which for a series of years opposed itself to his religious advancement was serious, and for the time fatal. It was this: He did not believe in the divinity of Jesus Christ; the divine in the human he did not comprehend, and not comprehending would not believe. He was not accustomed to accept what he did not understand, and this mystery was beyond the power of human intellect. I had frequent interviews with him, and can almost quote his exact words on this subject.

"I am not an infidel," he said, "I abhor the very name. I believe the Bible is a divinely-inspired book. Its precepts are of God. How could I believe otherwise when its moral influence is so good? I have often known bad men made good by becoming Christians, but never knew a good man made worse by being religious. If its influence is so universally good, then, sir, it commands the unqualified approval of my mind. I wish I could believe. Nothing would afford me so much pleasure as to be a member of the Church, and give to my children the benefit of a religious example. I go to your church, and I worship with you. When you praise God, my heart too unites in grateful emotions. When you pray, I join in the supplication; but when you worship Jesus Christ, my best efforts to follow you utterly fail. I regret this fact more than any one else possibly can, but I cannot help it. I would not discourage my wife in her religious views and enjoyments, nor would I throw the least obstacle in the way of my children, for I want them all to be religious. I have therefore carefully kept my doubts from every member of my family."

He was so anxious to overcome his doubts, and embrace conscientiously the faith and hope of the Christian; he was so fixed in his attention to the preaching of the gospel; he was so uniform in his attendance upon divine worship; and so deep was the interest with which he conversed on the subject of personal religion, that I was led to hope he had experienced regeneration by the Holy Spirit. More than two years ago I expressed to him this hope, and giving him some portions of Scripture to read, begged him at his leisure carefully to examine himself by them. In a few months he informed me that, according to the evidences of regeneration as expressed in the First Epistle of John, he was unconverted.

The anxiety which he felt continued to increase, until his solicitude led him freely to converse with such intelligent friends as he believed to be pious. On this subject he spoke from the deep earnestness of a feeling heart. He would not mention his doubts where he thought they would in any wise disturb the faith of a Christian, or afford a subterfuge for a worldly spirit, but he told them only to such as were established in the truth, and to such as he thought might be able to assist in their removal.

A highly-valued friend of his, now living in Augusta, appreciating his difficulties, and fully sympathizing with him in his troubles, placed in his hands a small volume called "The Christ of History." This he read with unusual interest. The line of argument adopted by its author produced a new train of thought in his mind. The divine humanity was not a problem to be solved by the intellect, but an inspired and revealed truth to be received upon faith. Christ was not the end of the law for righteousness to those who *understand*, but to those who *believe*. Religion is not an abstract theory, which speculative minds may accept or reject according to their own caprices. It is a great moral and spiritual force, to be felt in the heart and to be experienced in the life. The divinity of Christ involves the veracity of God; then the only question to be decided is this: "Is God manifest in the flesh revealed?" If so, it must be believed or God pronounced untrue. With such views as these, and with a heart deeply impressed with the infinite importance of the subject under investigation, and with earnest prayer for the Divine guidance, Gov. Cobb came directly to the Book of God for instruction. So deeply were his mind and heart imbued with the transcendent magnitude to his own soul of the interest involved that in four days and nights he read with care the writings of Matthew, Mark, Luke and John. While his mind grasped the divine testimony here given to the exclusion of all doubts, his heart yielded grateful homage to the "One Mediator between God and man, the man Christ Jesus."

Bear with me while I give you the particulars of the last private interview I ever enjoyed with him. It occurred the Sabbath after the change above alluded to.

In reply to a question I had just asked him, he said,

"I accept Jesus Christ as divine, as the anointed Saviour of man. My doubts on this subject have all gone."

"General," said I, "do you trust him as your Saviour?"

"I do sir," said he.

"Do you give to him," said I, "the adoring reverence, the worship of your *heart?*"

"I do," said he, with great emphasis.

"Then do you contemplate him with *heartfelt love?*" said I. For a moment his emotions prevented utterance, and then, with deep feeling, he replied,

"I *do*, sir."

I advanced toward him with extended hand, which he grasped. I said to him,

"I welcome you into the spiritual family of my Father, and greet you as a brother." His tears flowed freely while his expression was full of joy. I proposed a prayer of thanksgiving. We both knelt, and at the close of the devotion, his *Amen* was audible and emphatic. Turning to me and remaining on his feet, he said, with eyes frequently overflowing with tears as he spoke:

"For fifteen years I have been painfully anxious about my spiritual condition. Not a day of that time has passed without prayer. Sometimes I have been almost in despair, but now, sir, I am relieved. The burden has gone from my heart, and I enjoy the quiet and peace of one who reposes for safety on the strength and grace of the Son of God." I was deeply impressed with his unction and earnestness. He continued the conversation with great animation for a half hour longer, manifesting the holy fervor of a newly-regenerated soul.

Now, my congregation, having heard the reasons upon which I base my hope that our friend was in the exercise of saving faith, you will sympathize with me in the pious expectation of meeting him where "the wicked cease from troubling and the weary are at rest." Let us rejoice in his gain, and while we mourn our loss, we will not forget the divine admonition, "Be ye also ready, for in such an hour as ye think not, the Son of Man cometh."

The Rev. J. S. Key, D. D., pastor of the Mulberry Street Methodist Church, Macon, Georgia, then arose and addressed the audience for about half an hour. His line of thought lay in the special providences of God which seemed to lead to Gen. Cobb's conversion.

He spoke with much feeling, and narrated facts and incidents which had come to his knowledge in a long and intimate association with Gen. Cobb.

Funeral Address of Dr. J. S. Key.

I am sure you will pardon me dear friends, if I should seem to violate the proprieties of this solemn, sacred hour. Bear with me if I should depart from the order of exercises to which we have been accustomed on such occasions.

Perhaps some may think that it were wiser and more appropriate that we should gather in this venerable hall, and surrounding with reverend silence these mortal remains, surrender our hearts to the memories of the past and the inspirations of the present; but I owe a debt to duty and to God—to the living and the dead—a debt urgent and unavoidable, and that must be discharged just now. My silence would be treachery both to God and my friend.

I pray you understand me now. I come to the discharge of this duty solely as a minister of God. To other and fitter hands will be assigned the office of eulogium. To history and posterity are already committed the record of public services, the name and fame of the illustrious dead. To me and to these my reverend associates has been confided the priesthood of the altar; and we stand by this altar to-day, in the presence of this most appalling and heart-rending dispensation, to expound and explain—to pronounce the few sad, solemn words, "dust to dust, ashes to ashes;" and, standing thus, we implore the Infinite Ruler that he would shed over the gloom of this scene the light of immortal hope.

My heart is greatly relieved by the scriptural persuasion that "the Lord is with us;" and I bring to you the solid comforts and the sublime hopes of the Divine presence. The only solution of the perplexing problems of human experience and the only true peace are to be found in the assurance of an overruling, special, divine Providence. You must not separate God from the individual life and experience. He is "all and in all." He is seeking by all means to impress himself upon all that he has made. He is speaking to us, coming very near, unfolding himself, laboring to communicate himself to his children. Aye more, God Almighty is in the forefront of nations and communities and individuals, guiding, shaping and directing.

And now I bring you the consolations contained in the doctrine of the divine Fatherhood. You and I and all his children are ever in the mind and borne on the heart of our Father, God. The gift of his Son to suffer and to die was the expression of a Father's yearning love for imperiled children. The mission of the Holy Ghost is the putting forth of divine effort to lead the prodigal wanderers back to their abandoned home. And Providence itself is but the arrangement and shaping of the events of our life so as the more effectually to secure the return and safety of his children. Ah! here is the great fault of our lives and the great mistake of our judgment—that we see God so rarely and realize so little of his working.

Never in my life has this view of divine providence been so clearly illustrated, and so impressively presented as by the closing years and months of the life of the illustrious dead.

Dear sorrowing friends, you knew him not—friend as he was, loved and prized. You looked into that sunlit face; you felt the generous grasp of that ever-open hand; you hung upon the tones of that magic voice, and yet you understood him not. There was a department of his life of which you had no knowledge—a chapter of his daily experience read only by a few; and that was the department in which God was laboring to win and to save him. It was my valued privilege to be familiar with his heart, and to receive from his own lips from time to time the assurance of the perpetual working of this most gracious providence.

Bear with me now as I unfold it to you.

As my honored brother has told you, about fifteen years ago, in this city, as the great statesman stood by the dying couch of his venerable sire and received his dying benediction, God's Spirit smote him to the heart. He has been frequently heard to say that the first great conviction of his spiritual life was received in that solemn hour. It was God's time and God's chosen means. The dying patriarch had been an illustrious Christian character. The son, while neither professing nor practicing the piety of the father, had learned to love the purity of his heart and the beauty of his life; and venerated him all the more because in him he had an illustration of what grace could accomplish in fallen humanity. The death of such a man, and such a death as his, was both convincing and convicting. Calmly, without fear and triumphantly, he closed his life, testifying to the last, bearing witness to the truth. All hearts were moved, and our honored friend went forth with his heart pierced by the arrow of conviction.

Subsequent to that event, and but a few years

ago, the untimely death of a brother upon whom his heart was set aroused afresh his convictions and turned his thoughts with renewed concern to the subject of death and the preparation for it. Now it is that we begin to see God engaged, combining and harnessing providential events as so many agencies working together for the salvation of a soul. What influences more promising of success than those employed!—the veneration of a son for a pious father, and the love of a brother for a brother whose Christian character was commanding! The object aimed at was accomplished. He could not gainsay the testimony of such witnesses. He dare not deny the truth of the religion which they illustrated and adorned. And with all the aspirations of his heart he yearned for a character and life similar to theirs. Now it was that he turned to the reading of the Scriptures with so much concern—a practice that he continued with increasing interest to the day of his death. But now, too, it was that his great life-struggle began. You have heard of his lifelong misgiving of the Godhead of Christ. It rose upon him with most distracting and paralyzing power. In Christ alone was there offered any hope of pardon and peace; "There is no other name given under heaven among men whereby we must be saved," and yet on this only Saviour he could not rest, for he could not recognize him as divine. Oh the doubts, the distraction, the terror that tormented him!

But God never lost him; and through all these years of turmoil and strife—these years of wasting and desolation—his spirit was looking to God, and his praying was incessant. For the most part he bore this terrible burden alone. He feared to make it public. He shrank from being regarded a scoffer, for in his secret soul he believed religion true, and longed to put it on and wear it. The love he bore his family kept a seal upon his lips, lest his children might inherit his doubts, and with them his grief and struggle. To only a few sympathizing friends, and to them only in the most sacred confidence, did he disclose his difficulties. It was wise; and even in this silence we see the guiding of the hand of God. It kept his heart sealed to all but an ever-loving Father.

I well remember the relation that he gave me of his impressions and convictions on one occasion while stationed in Florida during the recent war.

It was his habit to attend regularly on the Sabbath services in the sanctuary. On the occasion referred to the supper of the Lord was spread and the followers of Christ invited to partake. One by one, friends and acquaintances and various members of his staff left him and approached the place of communion, until he was wellnigh left alone sitting in his pew. Now again the spirit of conviction revisited him. The memory of the sainted dead revived. The knowledge that part of his family were constant communicants, from all of whom he was separated, aroused him afresh, and he trembled in his seat. Never shall I forget the earnestness with which he said to me,

"Sir, never dismiss a congregation when you administer the holy sacrament. It is the most powerful preaching that you can furnish."

I cannot trace all the course of the divine dealing. Let me hurriedly group the closing acts. The bitter disappointments of the war—the wreck of fortunes—the blight of hopes—the chaos of the present and the apprehensions of the future—were all made tributary to the spiritual purposes of God. From all these his heart turned to find the only rest and satisfaction. He turned to God with prayer and Scripture-reading. Who will doubt the providence that spared him through the perils of the war and the disasters and depressions that followed it? Who can doubt the mission of that bosom-friend—their communions—and the giving of that volume which seemed to be God's final stroke in opening his heart to the entrance of the truth? See how busy he was—how frequent his conversations with ministers and pious friends! Oh it was God invisible, yet laying hold upon him and hurrying him to secure a preparation for that end so rapidly approaching. There was no premonition or presentiment of death, and yet he seemed to work as though he had it in his eye.

My last interview with my distinguished friend was memorable, and should be mentioned on this occasion. After giving most minutely a statement of his change of mind, together with the agencies employed to effect it, he made special mention of his change of feelings, and expressed his surprise with great emphasis that whereas all his life through he had carried a horror of death, he could now look on the grave and think of the dying hour with comparative satisfaction. Surely it was a change wrought by grace, for the fear of death is only destroyed by divine grace. After hearing this convincing testimony of his change of nature, I insisted that he owed to God, his family and himself the obligation to connect himself formally and publicly with the Church. He seemed not to be taken unawares; but promptly, as if the whole subject had been canvassed and settled, replied,

"My family are absent. They will not return until the Fall. I prefer to connect myself with the Baptist church of this city (Macon, Georgia), as my wife's membership is here; and when she returns I will most assuredly become a member."

He was not permitted to consummate his purpose, "God having provided some better thing for him." He whose eye had followed him, and whose hand had guided him, found him ready and took him. Let us rest in hope.

The Rev. Mr. Wm. Flinn, pastor of the Presbyterian church in Milledgeville, and formerly chaplain of Gen. Cobb's command, followed Dr. Key in an affectionate and interesting discourse, in which he sought to make manifest the kindliness of heart and true nobility of his former commander.

Address of Rev. Wm. Flinn.

This is no mere formal or hollow ceremonial which we are enacting; nor is it simply in obedience to the call of affection that we are here. We are engaged in the performance of a high and solemn duty. It devolves upon the living to record and commemorate the virtues of the noble and good who have gone from us. To neglect this would be to wrong both the living and the dead. It would be to withhold from the living the stimulus to virtue and goodness which noble examples furnish; and it would be to rob the dead of that which is their justest due. "The memory of the just is blest, but the name of the wicked shall rot." The fond hope of leaving behind us a memory which the good will cherish and bless is one of the highest motives to well-doing. Our name is, of all our possessions, most peculiarly our own, because it is of our own creation; and it is of all others the most precious, because it only is imperishable. Death strips us of all besides; this only remains, a part, and the best part, of our immortal selves. Hence, *A good name is rather to be chosen than great riches, and loving favor than silver and gold.* For at the last general assize, when God, our Maker and our Judge, shall render with impartial justice to every man according to his works, the prize of eternal life in His presence shall be awarded only to those who in this life made the attainment of immortal glory and honor their aim, and sought it by patient continuance in well-doing.

To honor, therefore, the memory of the good with appropriate ceremonies is to discharge the obligations of a sacred duty. It is to subserve the cause of virtue and truth, and to promote the highest interests of mankind. We thus gather up the virtues of those who have finished their course and treasure them away as sacred relics, which may serve as incentives to those who come after. Good men, though dead, are thus enabled still to speak. These solemnities to-day give voice and utterance to the virtues of our noble friend and fellow-citizen, whose eloquent lips are now sealed in death. May it serve to awaken in the heart of many a young man here present the resolve to emulate his virtues!

Seldom in a degenerate age is the opportunity afforded us of holding up for commendation, with so little qualification or reserve, the character of a public man as it is our privilege to do to-day. I do not say that the character of Gov. Cobb was without fault or blemish. That would be to deny that he was human, and would pass for the exaggeration of personal friendship, or, what is worse, for flattery. Doubtless he had his faults, but I leave it to those who take pleasure in such things to search them out and set them forth. We have, in common, the sad inheritance of a depraved nature. The most that the best men can do is to war resolutely against all that is weak or selfish or sinful within them, and hold it in check, while they foster and strengthen and exercise that which is noble and good and true, and secure, if possible, for these better principles the habitual control. The trophies which each one wins must be measured by his success in this warfare. Of our honored friend I state that which will be conceded by all who knew him—that, measured by this rule, he was entitled to no common distinction.

Gifted with powers such as are bestowed upon but comparatively few men, he neither buried them in ignoble indolence and ease, nor prostituted them to the service of a narrow and selfish ambition, but he faithfully used them in the service of his country. Most of his life was spent in the public service, in obedience to the call of his fellow-citizens; and of the distinguished ability and fidelity with which he discharged his trust I need not speak.

His death is felt to be a public calamity, and it is appropriate that all classes should meet and mingle their tears at his tomb. Our country feels deeply his loss in this her hour of darkness. His far-reaching, comprehensive views as a statesman; his sound judgment; his wisdom and prudence in counsel; his noble, conciliatory spirit and true magnanimity; his steady, unflinching fortitude in maintaining the cause of truth and right; his cheerful patience under the burdens of our common calamities,—all united to make him a leader to whom we looked up; and now that he is gone it is as if a great light had been extinguished, and the world has grown darker and the gloom around us has gathered thicker in consequence.

In his death the poor have lost a friend. The tears of many a widow and fatherless child will flow freely and bitterly when they listen to the announcement of his death; and the blessing of him that was ready to perish, relieved by his hand, shall rest upon his memory. His kindness to the poor was generous and catholic and, in general, did not stop to regard character or color. If the applicant was in want, he inquired no farther, but promptly relieved him. I have in my mind's eye at this moment an aged and helpless negro woman, formerly his slave, who since her freedom has been indebted to his indulgent kindness for a neat and comfortable home and a liberal supply for all her wants. It was his habit, when called by business to Milledgeville, where she lives, to visit her, inquire kindly into her affairs and see that she was in need of nothing. On his last visit to her I accompanied him, and was an eye-witness to his generous care of one who could not possibly make him any return.*

* Old Aunt Jenny Lamar, an original African, died last week at probably about ninety years of age. She was a servant of Col. Zach. Lamar, who, in his will, in consideration of her kindness to his family, gave her a house and lot in this city, and required that his daughter, Mrs. Gen. Cobb, should support her as long as she lived, and exact no service of her. The wishes of her master were faithfully carried out, and she lived, for more than thirty years, at the home thus provided for her, where her wants were supplied and a girl kept to wait on her. She was a good, Christian woman, and white and black entertained for her the kindest feeling.—*Milledgeville* (*Ga.*) *paper*, *July*, 1869.

The Church will feel his loss. When our blessed Lord was on earth he was once approached by the elders of the Jews in behalf of a Roman centurion who desired a favor. *When they came to Jesus they besought him instantly, saying, That he was worthy for whom He should do this: for he loveth our nation and hath built us a synagogue.* So Gov. Cobb, though not a member of the Church by formal profession, or by the reception of the sealing ordinances of our holy religion, yet was a friend to the Church. He habitually exhibited a profound respect for all that pertained to our Christianity. He was a constant attendant upon the preaching of the gospel, a liberal and cheerful contributor to the support of its ministry, and an earnest student of its profoundest mysteries. The ministers of religion found in him a generous friend. He honored them for the Master's sake, and he gave much more than the cup of cold water to relieve their wants. Their wants were relieved and their hearts made glad by his liberal bounty, bestowed with inimitable delicacy.

Indulge me while I speak something from personal recollection of my honored and cherished friend. I knew him well. I was associated with him intimately under circumstances of peculiar trial. I was his chaplain and messmate in the army. I saw him and conversed with him daily in all the unrestrained intimacy of confiding friendship. We exchanged views on almost every subject which could interest the human mind. I may claim therefore to know him, if one man can know another—to know his sentiments and principles and habits. And I utter what I now say in all solemnity: I do not recollect ever to have heard him utter a sentiment which was dishonorable. I never saw him do an act to any human being which I thought unjust or even unkind. I never knew him to neglect an opportunity of doing a kindness, for it seemed to be the natural impulse of his heart. I never heard him utter a word of bitterness in resentment for what he considered a personal wrong. I know that he did utter words of withering bitterness sometimes, but they were directed against what he considered falsehood, duplicity or meanness; they were not in resentment of personal offences. Magnanimous, truthful, frank and generous in every impulse of his nature, he scorned and loathed their opposites in others, and he denounced them with all the fervor of his warm heart. It affords me pleasure to be able to bear this testimony to this noble characteristic of that good man. Indeed, in my great admiration of his character and my warm affection for the man, I used to say of him in my heart, making due allowance for the infirmities of our common nature, *One thing only thou lackest.* And it gave me a joy which I cannot utter when I learned that, by the sovereign grace of God, that one thing had been supplied, and that he had been led by a humble, simple faith to lay hold of that hope which is set before us in the gospel.

But it has pleased God in his wisdom to take him away from us. We must now bear his honored remains, and deposit them, with sorrowing hearts and tearful eyes, in the house appointed for all living. And then we must turn away with the mournful conviction that we shall see his face no more and not again hear his voice on earth. But we confidently hope to meet him in a better land, and amid brighter scenes.

Let this be our comfort for the present.

[The following interesting address was prepared for the funeral occasion of Gov. Cobb by Dr. Brantly, formerly Professor of Belles Lettres and

Oratory in the University of Georgia, who, in common with the other clergymen, had been invited to officiate; but the length of time to which the exercises had been prolonged precluded its delivery. It was, however, procured by the editor of this volume, and he publishes it as a part of the proceedings, believing that it will add to the interest of these records.]

Address of Rev. Wm. T. Brantly, D. D.

My brethren to whom you have just listened have enlarged in fitting terms on the virtues and services of our friend whose remains are in the coffin before us. Whilst we mourn that his noble intellect has suffered the eclipse of death, it is grateful to remember that its active powers once adorned those eminent positions which his countrymen called him to fill in his own State, in the halls of our National Councils, in the Cabinet and in the Field. It is interesting, too, to hear of those deeds of generosity and philanthropy to which he was moved by a heart in earnest sympathy with his species. Above all, it is good to be assured that the spirit which has gone to God who gave it, has departed clothed in that spotless robe without which no fallen being can appear acceptably before his Maker.

But whilst we eulogize our departed brother, our solicitude should be awakened lest this afflictive occurrence be without practical benefit to those by whom he was esteemed and loved. If we fail to ponder the lesson of our own mortality, and to consider the importance of habitual preparation for that solemn event which is inevitable, and which may confront us "in such an hour as we think not," then, so far as we are concerned, his death will be a vanity. The associations of this place combine with the mournful dispensation which has convened us to-day to speak with unwonted emphasis of the necessity of being ready for that summons to which we must all respond. General Cobb was for more than twenty-five years a Trustee of this University. As I recur to the public occasions when I have seen him sitting on this rostrum from which I now address you, I am reminded of the manly forms which once, with his, occupied these seats, and who with him have taken their places in the silent halls of death. Each speaks, though dead, and announces the mortality of those who survive. Of the twenty-eight gentlemen who constituted the Board of Trustees of the College at the time of Gen. Cobb's election, but seven remain; and some of these are so aged and feeble that it is manifest their departure from earth cannot be long postponed. A fifth of a century has just passed since I became officially connected with this College. In this period I have seen more than twenty of those who were at different times associated with our friend in guarding the interests of the institution, disappear from the ranks of the living. What an impressive illustration of the vanity of human life!

The very last time I had occasion to speak in this chapel was in response to an invitation to commemorate the life and services of one who, whilst he was a member of this Board, dignified the ermine of the highest judicial position in the State. Not many years before his removal the Board was bereaved by the loss of that patriotic and gallant son of the State who fell on the hotly-contested field of Sharpsburg. Though but a brother by marriage, LAMAR was, in tenderness and devotion, all that a brother according to the flesh could be to him for whom we are this day mourning. Only a few months prior to this painful casualty, Georgia had mourned the loss of that Christian soldier and self-sacrificing patriot, the younger Cobb, who in the very hour of a victory largely won by his own gallant band, yielded up his life on the bloody slopes of Fredericksburg.

As I unroll the records of the score of years to which I have referred, other forms familiar and beloved present themselves. I see the lamented Harden, who for more than a third of a century was a faithful sentinel over the interests of this University, beginning his services at a time of the utmost depression, and continuing them until the efforts of himself and his colleagues were crowned with large success; I see Berrien, whose golden-mouthed oratory made him the very Chrysostom of the Bar and of the Senate, whilst his dignified carriage was worthy of a Roman Senate in the palmiest days of its history; and Harris, who for a protracted period gave to the Board the benefit of his sagacious counsels, cherishing this College with a paternal devotion, and rejoicing in its success as he would exult over the prosperity of his own child; and Towns, the constant friend and genial companion, for four years Chief Magistrate of Georgia, but cut down in the very prime of his manhood; and FORT, so long the ornament of the Medical profession of the State, winning the confidence and the love of all who were so fortunate as to know him; and GILMER, also honored with the highest office which the people of his adopted State could confer upon him; and SCHLEY, holding successively the offices of Judge, Congressman and Governor—a man who was ever ready to "swear to his own hurt and change not," one before whose honest eye deceit and fraud retired abashed; and HAMILTON, faithfully and freely bestowing upon the College those prudent counsels by which he had achieved such distinguished success in the enterprises of business to which his life was devoted; and McDONALD, of whom, though a kinsman, I may be permitted to say a more honest and unselfish politician, a purer patriot and a more judicious adviser is not found in the long list of Georgia's gifted and illustrious sons. On this record appears the name still further of DAWSON, always cordial, always popular, with malice for none, with a kind word for all, filling with distinction the high positions to which he was called in the councils of the State and country; and MERCER, sustaining with becoming dignity the reputation of a great and good name; and WAYNE, who for a full half century was connected with this Board—at the time of his decease the oldest member, and its only Representative in the Supreme Court of the Republic; and WINGFIELD—the amiable, gentle, hospitable, courteous Wingfield—whose politeness was in his day a proverb, because his heart overflowed with the milk of human kindness. I have seen all these names stricken from the roll by the unsparing hand of the ruthless Effacer. As each one has passed away he has but increased the already "great cloud of witnesses" to the grand fact of our mortality.

Nor do I forget at this time those colleagues of the departed Cobb who, like himself, were removed instantaneously from earthly scenes. I recall now the ingenuous countenance, the noble brow of the gifted DOUGHERTY, who, at nearly the same age and by the same disease, was swept away in the full tide of health—hurried from the manly sports of the field in which at the time he was indulging. ELLIOT, too, occurs to my mind. How often have I seen his imperial form on this stage! Majestic in person, vigorous and well-balanced in intellect, truly pious and catholic in spirit, he seemed to be one foreordained to hold eminent position in the Church of Christ. But his gifts nor his graces could delay the approach of the inexorable Summoner. He returned to his home from a parochial visitation but to hear the call which transferred him in a moment from the Church militant to the Church triumphant. Well, too, do I remember HULL. How sudden his dismissal from the body! Like Wayne, he was for full fifty years connected with this Board; and during this entire period he was, as an officer and a man, the very embodiment of fidelity and integrity. Having finished the morning devotions of the family, he awaited, with the open Bible before him, the summons to the morning repast. When addressed he returned no response. The breakfast lay untasted on the table, whilst he went to enjoy the feast which the Saviour in whom he trusted had prepared for him in the realms of the blest. He departed, leaving that "good name which is better than precious ointment, and more to be chosen than great riches." Nor must I omit from the necrology of the period under review the name of him who for so many years presided over the meetings of this Board and over the University. My nearest neighbor and constant associate for eight years, I knew him well. So long as a conscientious devotion to duty, disdaining all ease and self-indulgence in the presence of its claims, can entitle a man to the commendation of his fellow-citizens, so long as a courage which knew no blenching in the presence of difficulties however formidable can awaken admiration, so long as piety, simple, earnest, uniform, deserves to be eulogized, the name of ALONZO CHURCH should be cherished by those to whom he devoted the best efforts of his intellect and the warmest affections of his heart.

And now to this constantly-growing catalogue of the dead we add the name of the elder COBB. He too is smitten down full of honors, though not full of years. He was as yet in the full vigor of his manhood, and it was fondly hoped that he might live for many years to bless the country with his matured experience and his patriotic counsels. But he had reached the "appointed bounds." He feels the icy touch of the Destroyer upon his vitals; in an instant consciousness departs, and almost with the unfinished sentence upon his lips "the wind passes over him and he is gone." Oh! as we look around and see other occupants of these seats, where we have so often greeted the honored curators of this University, we cannot repress the exclamation of the royal Psalmist: "Our days on the earth are as a shadow, and there is none abiding." Exposed as we all are to the remorseless scythe of that enemy before whom so many "tall and wise and reverend heads" have fallen, how important is it to clothe ourselves with that panoply by which we may be assured of triumph in the conflict. Thank God, that victory is possible! Blessed be his Name, that with faith in him we can respond to the citation which calls us from earth, not

> "Like the quarry slave forced to his dungeon,
> But like one that wraps the drapery of his couch about him
> And lies down to pleasant dreams."

If we are roused by the providence which converts this chapel into a house of mourning to consider our own mortality with something of that seriousness which the subject demands, the occasion, though afflictive, will be salutary. We shall thus confirm the declaration of the wise man, that "it is better to go to the house of mourning than to the house of feasting; for that is the end of all men, and the living will lay it to his heart."

Dr. Brantly offered the following

PRAYER.

Father of our spirits and Framer of our bodies! We desire to recognize thee in the dispensation which fills our hearts with sorrow and our eyes with tears to-day. "Before the mountains were brought forth, or ever thou hadst formed the earth and the world, even from everlasting to everlasting thou art God." "Thou turnest man to destruction and sayest, Return, ye children of men." Thou dost breathe into our nostrils the breath of life. Thou dost cause these hearts to throb and these lungs to heave and play; and when thou dost order it, they are silent and still. At thy command we die and return to dust. "As for us, O God, our days are as grass; as flowers of the field, so we flourish; for the wind passes over us and we are gone; and the places thereof shall know us no more." But we do praise thee that though we are changing and dying, thou art the same and thy years shall never fail. We thank thee that thou dost invite us to look away from the corruption and gloom of death, assured that they who trust in thee can never die. Thou art showing us to-day that "there is but a step between us and death"—that we "know not what a day may bring forth." We pray that we may all be aroused by this affecting illustration of the uncertainty of life to make without delay (if hitherto it has been neglected) that preparation which is necessary to a peaceful meeting with thee.

We thank thee that we have reason to believe that the blow which fell so suddenly on our departed brother did not find him destitute of this preparation. We bless thee for the testimony which we have heard from successive witnesses that, being justified by faith, he possessed peace with thee. Holy Spirit, we praise thee that thou didst dissipate the blindness of unbelief and error, and didst bring him, though after a season of much anxiety and struggling and prayer, to rely on the Lamb's atoning blood. Glory to thy name, thou God of long-suffering and forbearance, that we are not left in ignorance concerning this one who is asleep, sorrowing as for one for whom there is no hope.

And now, O Lord, let it please thee to hear us in behalf of the bereaved survivors. We desire especially to commend unto thee that one who is most deeply smitten by this visitation of thy hand. Look upon her in "her affliction and her pain." Thou seest how, even in the midst of fond and loving hearts, she feels alone in the world. Thou hast taken away "the desire of her eyes." Thou hast deprived her of the companion and husband of her youth; and thou dost compel her to say in the deep poignancy of her grief, "Lover and friend hast thou put far from me, and mine acquaintance into darkness." O sympathizing Jesus, thou who didst weep with the mourning sisters at a brother's grave, extend to her thine own precious sympathies and succors. Fulfill in her experience the gracious promise that her strength shall be as her days. Help her to believe and to feel that the chastening now upon her, bitter, grievous though it be, is but a part of that discipline which a Saviour wise and merciful employs to educate his child for that place which he has gone before to prepare for her. Help her in the midst of her distress and anguish to say, not only "the Lord gave and the Lord has taken away," but to add with the spirit of perfect acquiescence, "blessed be the name of the Lord."

Hear us for these sons and daughters who are

weeping together around the coffin of a loving and tender father. May they now, O God, find in thee a friend who can more than supply the place of the fondest earthly parent—who is willing to do, and who has promised to do for those who call on his name, more than earthly parents in the largest exercise of their affection can bestow. Hear us for these brothers and sisters who are made common mourners to-day. Though they can mingle no more in the scenes where they have so often met the beloved one for whom they mourn, may they be comforted with the hope of meeting again in that better land where the parting word is never spoken and the parting tear is never shed!

Give us all such a use of this event that we may *earnestly* seek to be ready for the Son of man whenever he may come!

Almighty God, we thank thee that though we now dwell in the land of the dying, there is a land of the living—a place where there shall be no more suffering, nor sorrow, nor sin, nor death, nor mourning. Assist us to look away from this "tabernacle in which we now groan, being burdened, to the building of God, the house not made with hands, eternal in the heavens." Give us such faith, such consecration to thy service, that each one may say with thine ancient servant, "For me to live is Christ"—so that we may also say with him, "to die is gain." And to thy name, Father, Son, and Holy Spirit, be the glory, world without end. Amen.

The solemn funeral service was continued by Bishop Heber's beautiful hymn, "Thou art gone to the grave," which was read by Rev. F. H. Ivey, Pastor of the Athens (Georgia) Baptist Church.

Farewell to a Friend Departed.

Thou art gone to the grave; but we will not deplore thee,
Though sorrows and darkness encompass the tomb;
The Saviour has passed through its portals before thee,
And the lamp of his love is thy guide through the gloom.

Thou art gone to the grave; we no longer behold thee,
Nor tread the rough paths of the world by thy side;
But the wide arms of mercy are spread to enfold thee,
And sinners may hope, since the Saviour hath died.

Thou art gone to the grave; and, its mansion forsaking,
Perchance thy weak spirit in doubt lingered long;
But the sunshine of heaven beamed bright on thy waking,
And the sound thou didst hear was the seraphim's song.

Thou art gone to the grave; but we will not deplore thee,
Since God was thy Ransom, thy Guardian, thy Guide;
He gave thee, he took thee, and he will restore thee;
And death has no sting since the Saviour hath died.

As the last sad notes of the hymn died away, the wreath-covered coffin was borne forth and transported to the cemetery, followed by thousands. There, surrounded by weeping friends and relatives, it was consigned to the tomb.

Rev. E. W. Warren read a short selection from the Bible, and offered a brief, but solemn prayer, and then the grave closed upon all that was mortal of Howell Cobb.

The sun was just sinking beneath the western horizon, and, as the large assembly slowly and sadly dispersed, the shades of evening gathered over the scene—fit emblem of the sadness which shrouded the spirits of all.

Shortly after the funeral the following appeared in one of the journals of the State, and is given as a spontaneous exemplification of the feeling caused in Georgia by the death of Howell Cobb:

One month ago, a mighty heart beat high,
Tumultuous throbbings, rending to and fro,
Alternate hope and fear, like lightning's stroke
Upon a giant oak—*he fell at morn;*
And as the wingèd messenger the tidings bore,
How was the land he loved in mourning clad!
Georgia—the inspiration of his life and lips—
Felt the deep wound in her sad mother-heart;
And as I saw him on her bosom laid,

After such tears upon his bier were shed
As man might covet, but not often claim;
And loving hearts forgot "the *great man*" there,
To call him "friend and brother," and God's messengers
Brought comfort for the living in his death,
Because he had received "into his heart
God's kingdom"—even "as a little child,"
And so "had entered in." After all these
Kindly and sacred tributes to the dead,
I saw the earth receive him, and I thought
Could aught make her cold bosom *throb with life*,
'Twas touch of patriot dust upon her soil!
But if unconscious of her precious charge,
The river, where his boyish footsteps strayed
Makes soothing murmur round his resting-place;
And trees that grew apace with his own growth
Will shelter lovingly *two sacred mounds*
Where brothers rest—"divided not in death"—
Beneath the sunshine of their native land—
Immortal brothers in each Southern heart!

Lines to the Memory of Gen. Cobb.

BY E. B. C.

Slow, loitering Time,
Thou canst not cheat sweet memory of her debt!
No, no! her loving hand upon us yet
Is nestling. Bleeding hearts cannot forget
Their thoughts sublime.

Yes, wounded hearts,
Your dark and ruined home before our eyes
For ever is. The picture never dies;
But in the depths of sadden'd souls it lies,
And ne'er departs.

The proudest son,
The noblest, truest patriot Georgia bore,
Our country's sinking ark can guide no more.
He stands a glowing vision on *that shore*,
His work well done!

Thou hast the power,
O God, from out the foaming surge, the deep,
The mad, the bitter waves to lead, and keep
Within thy wing these trembling ones who weep
And mourn that hour.

Look down upon
Thy blighted ones, O Father God, to-day,
And in thy spirit clothe them that they may
All see thy power—all love it—Lord, all say,
"Thy will be done!"

MACON, GEORGIA, 1869.

HONORS.

The memory of the just is blessed.—Proverbs x. 7.

I've scanned the actions of his daily life
With all the industrious malice of a foe;
And nothing meets mine eye but deeds of honor.

The honors of a name 'tis just to guard;
They are a trust but lent us, which we take,
And should, in reverence to the donor's fame,
With care transmit them down to other hands.

Lives of all great men remind us
  We can make our lives sublime,
And, departing, leave behind us
  Footprints on the sands of time—
Footsteps, that perhaps another,
  Sailing o'er life's solemn main,
A forlorn and shipwreck'd brother,
  Seeing, shall take heart again.

IV.

HONORS.

THE following is the action taken by the Bar of the United States Circuit Court for the Southern District of Georgia, when that Court was sitting in Savannah, in November, 1868:

RESOLUTIONS OF RESPECT FOR THE MEMORY OF THE LATE HON. HOWELL COBB.

SAVANNAH, November 6, 1868.

In pursuance of the adjournment yesterday, the Bar of the United States Circuit Court for the Southern District of Georgia assembled in the Court-room this morning, at three-quarters past nine o'clock, Hon. E. A. Nisbet in the chair.

The Committee of five appointed yesterday, through General A. R. Lawton, their Chairman, reported the following resolutions:

Resolved, That in the death of the Hon. Howell Cobb the State of Georgia has lost one of the ablest, purest and most patriotic of her citizens, who, as her Representative in the National Councils, as her Chief Executive Magistrate, and in the high Cabinet position, exhibited a comprehensive grasp of intellect, an intuitive quickness of perception, and practical directness of thought which had enrolled his name among the most eminent American statesmen; and who, by a long career of useful and self-devoting service, has enshrined his memory in the hearts of her people.

Resolved, That in this afflicting dispensation of Providence, we mourn the loss of a professional brother, endowed with a rare capacity as a counselor and advocate; of a companion and friend, the truthfulness, nobility and expansive sympathies of whose nature, and the vivacious play of whose intellect could not fail to endear him to all who knew him well, or to make him the radiating centre of the social circle.

Resolved, That we respectfully tender to his beloved family our sincerest sympathy and profoundest condolence in their sad bereavement.

Resolved, That these proceedings be published

in the gazettes of this city, and a copy be furnished to the family of the deceased.

The resolutions were unanimously adopted, and the meeting adjourned *sine die*.

E. A. Nisbet, Chairman.

Wm. S. Basinger, Secretary.

Proceedings of the Macon Bar.

Life and Character of Howell Cobb.

A few days subsequent to the death of Gov. Cobb, the Macon Bar, of which he was an honored member, convened and appointed a committee to prepare a suitable tribute to the memory of their distinguished brother. This task devolved upon Hon. E. A. Nisbet, chairman of the committee, and on the first of December, 1868, the Bibb County Superior Court being in session, Judge E. B. Cole presiding, the committee made its report.

Hon. E. A. Nisbet, before reading the report, said: It has been my duty, during a long professional life, to pay tribute to the memory of many deceased members of the Bar, but I have been called upon on no occasion more peculiar and sadder than the present. There are circumstances in relation to the death of Gen. Cobb which distinguish it from any other within my experience. His distinction as a politician both before and since the war, his high grade as a lawyer, his amiable character and numerous social virtues, and the place and manner of his death, all combine to increase the solemnities of this occasion. He died suddenly in the city of New York—the great theatre of events, of observation and excitement—with the eyes of the nation upon the melancholy event; but, sir, inasmuch as it has been my duty, as chairman of the committee, to sketch in outline the prominent traits of his character, I forbear, and shall content myself with reading the report of the committee, and adding that his life is a brilliant example for imitation, and his death an illustration of the beautiful teachings of the British poet—

> The boast of heraldry, the pomp of power,
> And all that beauty, all that wealth e'er gave,
> Await alike the inevitable hour:
> The paths of glory lead but to the grave.

The committee appointed to prepare a suitable tribute to the memory of the late Gen. Cobb, beg leave to submit the following:

General Howell Cobb, being on a visit to the

North, with his wife and daughter, died in the city of New York, on the ninth day of October last, at the age of fifty-three years. He was seized suddenly, was prostrated in a moment of time and expired in a few minutes thereafter. A man of vigorous constitution and, until very recently, in the enjoyment of uninterrupted health, no one had a fairer promise of long life; and surrounded with numerous and devoted friends, and blessed with the sweetest and richest endearments of home and family, of a life of unmingled happiness. He was called hence without premonition. This providence, to our limited vision, looks strange; but we well know that it is not for us to sit in judgment upon the inscrutable events of the Divine government. We believe that the all-wise and all-merciful Ruler ordereth all things well, and, therefore, it is our duty and privilege to acquiesce without a murmur in His dispensations. "Justice and judgment are the habitation of thy throne; mercy and truth shall go before thy face." When the telegraph announced the death of our brother, thousands of people all over this broad land—and we among the number—felt that they had lost a loved and cherished personal friend. The country was stricken with awe and tremulousness. Sadness and sorrow and deep regrets fell upon all who knew him. We may not assume to speak of the effects of their great bereavement upon the family of the deceased. *They* have solved the mystery of unutterable grief. And yet, as we shall see, even they are not left to mourn as those who have no hope. It is a melancholy pleasure for us to honor the name and memory of Gen. Cobb. Alas! how melancholy! Still it is a pleasure. It is indeed pleasant to be enabled to place upon the records of this Court our unanimous, cordial, unqualified testimony to his genius and learning, his professional honor, his statesmanship, his patriotism, his kindness of heart and his unrivaled social attractiveness. We lay this offering upon his tomb. It may be humble, but it expresses our affection and our respect for his character as eloquently as would a monument carved in marble and emblazoned with gold.

Gen. Cobb was a native of Georgia, born of highly respectable and pious parents in the county of Jefferson. He was graduated at the University of Georgia, during the Presidency of Dr. Church, in the class of 1834. Immediately after his graduation he commenced the study of the law under the direction of Gen. Hardin, a most excellent gentleman of that ilk, and when admitted, at an early age, settled in the town of Athens, Clarke county. Very soon he acquired a good practice, both in his own county and in the circuit. For several years he held the office of Solicitor-General of the Western Circuit, discharging its duties efficiently, zealous to convict the guilty, but forbearing toward the innocent.

Neither the sovereignty of the State nor the citizen suffered wrong at his hands. A brilliant career awaited him. With a commanding person, fine voice, conciliatory address, industry, thorough mental furniture; ardent, self-reliant, ambitious, he would have speedily reached the highest level of professional distinction. But a change came over the spirit of his dream, and like most young men of that day who were conscious of intellectual power, he became enamored of political life, and his aspirations in that direction were so promptly realized that his profession became an object of secondary importance.

After the fall of the Confederate Government, he settled in the city of Macon and resumed the practice. His success was equal to his most sanguine expectations; clients multiplied, and at his death he stood in the front rank of the Georgia Bar. Upon an occasion so solemn as this it becomes us to say nothing for effect and to indulge in no exaggeration; and we may, therefore, hope that our estimate of Gen. Cobb, professionally and otherwise, will be taken as true and candid. He was not, in legal arguments, a dealer in dull, dusty cases, with little or no application to the point at issue. He was master of the principles of our noble science, and his acute discrimination and clear, vigorous judgment enabled him to apply them successfully. Nor did he rely upon them and his native originating power alone, but was wont to arm himself with authority—that latest authority which ruled the principle and most perspicuously illustrated it. His manner of argumentation was logical, without the stiff, cold formality of scholasticism. Indeed he was a natural logician: he knew well how to assume premises and draw conclusions without the aid of the syllogism or the tricks of the sophist. Before the Court he had great power of condensation, and never weakened his cause by repetition or profuse elaboration. He was happy in the handling of facts before the jury, and skillful, though fair, in his statement of them—just to his adversary, earnest and persuasive, not unfrequently wielding at will both the convictions and the passions of the panel. In this connection, it may be proper to say that his eloquence found its happiest display before large popular assemblies. He was peculiarly at home at the hustings: there he achieved his most splendid triumphs—there he became regal. His clarion voice reached the ear of a great multitude, and his honest, amiable character reached their hearts.

Gen. Cobb's political career was not only successful, but exceedingly brilliant. He rose rapidly from one position to another, until he became a recognized leader of the great Democratic party of the American Union. This is not the occasion, nor ours the duty, to trace his ascending course. That responsible task will devolve upon the historian or the biographer. Suffice it now to say that, before the war, he represented his district in Congress for a number of years; was Speaker of the House of Representatives; Governor of Georgia; and Secretary of the Treasury during Mr. Buchanan's administration. His political record may be said to be voluminous. In it there is not to be found a blot or a blur. Amidst all the violence of party warfare no one of his political opponents, however unscrupulous, was ever known to utter a word impugning his integrity as an officer or his honor as a gentleman. The House of Representatives of the United States is a theatre upon whose boards demagogues play for popularity, partisans for power, genius and eloquence for renown, and patriots for peace, order and good government. It is, therefore, often disorderly, and frequently tumultuous. To preside over such a body with acceptability requires rare endowments —a thorough knowledge of men—quickness of perception — patience — self-control — firmness —a clear sense of justice—tact and impartiality.

Especially is it necessary that the officer command the respect of the house. That is, in fact, the chief element of his authority. All these qualities our friend possessed in an eminent degree; and hence it was that no speaker, since the time of Mr. Clay, discharged the duties of the chair with more marked efficiency than did he. When the State seceded, having contributed as much to that result as any other citizen, he gave himself unconditionally to the cause of the South. He yielded to it all the honors which he had won under the Union, and consecrated to its success his name, his estate and his life. He was elected a member of the Provisional Congress, and when it met was chosen its presiding officer. No body ever convened at the South was more able or more patriotic than this Congress. Party prepossessions, committals, animosities and creeds had no place in the deliberations of that august assembly. They could not live in an atmosphere charged with the sublime responsibilities of a stupendous revolution. A constitution was passed upon the basis of the principles of 1776, which was an improvement, as many believe, upon the Federal Constitution; laws were passed and officers chosen to administer them. The civil revolution was in a few weeks accomplished, and the new government moved forward with a harmonious grandeur unparalleled in the annals of empire. To these ends no member contributed more than Gen. Cobb. His experience, profound knowledge of constitutional law, his devotion to constitutional liberty and his sound judgment, were all made available in that great crisis. He was also a member of the permanent Confederate Congress; but when the war began to rage, with its terrific foreshadowing of slaughter, poverty and the scaffold, he retired from the halls of legislation and joined the army, rising rapidly to the grade of major-general. In the military service he was ever prudent, obedient to rightful authority, gallant and energetic. When the Confederate Government—after sacrifices indescribable and the display of heroism unimagined in the wildest dream of romance—fell, he conceded the fact of its extinction by overwhelming force, and acquiesced in the necessity of the surrender of its armies.

Not only so, but he advised and urged the return of the Southern States to their former place in the Union. Uncomplainingly, and with quiet dignity, he retired to the walks of private life. We looked to him in these latter-day troubles and in the contingencies of the future as one of our wisest, safest advisers. We did well hope that he would live to be, as he ever had been, the champion of law and liberty. But he has passed "from gloom to glory," and his country has nothing left but the heritage of his fame and virtues.

Turn we now to contemplate him in his private

character. A mere outline sketch is all that we are at liberty to appropriate to a theme to which a volume might well be devoted. Its necessary meagreness, however, does not make it otherwise than grateful. It is sometimes the case that eminent men, especially in political life, draw around them friends from fear, or favor, or policy. Gov. Cobb's friends became such from affection. It is believed that he left more personal friends than any man who has lived and died in the State. These admired him for his ability, but loved him for the kindness, generosity and nobility of his nature. They were attracted by his stern sense of justice, by his benevolence, his charity and his genial companionship. Had he been less distinguished, he would not have been less beloved.

Political antagonism engendered no bitterness in his soul, rivalry created no hatred, and disappointment did not lessen his cheerfulness. Public life did not cool the warmth of his heart, and high position did not weaken in him the obligation of social duties. Nor was he capricious in his likings, but true and staunch through evil and through good report. The lowly and the lofty alike, if meritorious, shared in his good offices and elicited his sympathy.

In the relations of husband, parent, brother and companion, he was a model man. His intercourse with his family was governed by the law of love.

As its head he ruled with prudence and authority, but it was the authority of superior wisdom, united with forbearance, tenderness and assiduous attention. His wife and children alone know, and they only can tell, how sweet were the charities of their home.

The soldiers of his command during the war testify to his considerate attention. The poor, the suffering and dying were always the objects of his care and kindness. It has been represented recently by one occupying a high place, that he visited upon a sick and dying Federal prisoner extreme and wanton cruelty. This charge has been conclusively disproved, but if it were not, we who knew him well, could not, would not believe it. It is contradicted by the whole tenor of his life, and by the unbroken course of our experience of his character. And, standing as we do at the brink of his recently-opened grave, we take the responsibility of saying that the conduct attributed to him was utterly impossible.

Perhaps in nothing was the goodness of his heart more beautifully manifested than in his benevolent attention to dependants—some of the old and faithful servants, for example, of the family. These he provided for and protected. Destitution and want always drew from him sympathy and supplies.

It remains to speak of his religious character. He never made a public profession of religion, but it is known to his intimate friends that he had made up his mind to unite with the Baptist Church—the Church of his parents and of his wife—upon his return this fall to Macon. In the judgment of those friends he died a Christian. And this is the hope that, we trust, even now mitigates the sorrow of his mourning family and relations, and will, ere long, reconcile them to his loss. He was a praying man for fifteen years before his death, according to his own account, but was harassed with doubts about the divinity of the Saviour—that is, as to the Godhead dwelling in the humanity of Christ. He could not solve the mystery of Godliness—God manifest in the flesh—which the Scriptures themselves pronounce great. Unable to believe without a satisfactory comprehension of this fundamental truth of our holy religion, he did not, until lately, enjoy a sensible realization of pardon and peace. This kind of struggle of a strong mind to subject revelation to the authority of reason is not uncommon. No doubt it is hard for one accustomed to think, analyze and understand, to become as a little child—a learner at the foot of the cross. But subordinating his pride of intellect and pride of life to a simple effort of faith, and inspired by the Holy Spirit, a careful study of the Scriptures resulted in a sense of acceptance with God. He became the recipient of that purest, best and most sublime blessing ever vouchsafed to humanity—regeneration. And thus anointed, sanctified and accepted, his spirit entered rest—that rest which shall endure through eternal ages.

"O Gracious God! not gainless is our loss:
A glorious sunbeam gilds thy sternest frown:
And while his country staggers with the cross,
He rises with the crown."

Resolved, That this Bar, his country and his family have sustained a great bereavement in the death of Gen. Howell Cobb; that he was endeared to us by his manly, generous, cordial professional companionship and association; to his country by his sacrifices and services, and to his family by his tender affection, his considerate providence and his wise counsels; that we deplore that one so dear to us and so full of the promise of future usefulness should be called hence in the full maturity of all his powers: satisfied, however, that our loss is his great gain, we do not question the wisdom and mercy of God in transferring his spirit from earth to heaven.

2. *Resolved,* That our respectful sympathy and condolence are hereby tendered to his family.

3. *Resolved,* That the members of this Bar will wear crape on the left arm for the time of thirty days, as a testimonial of our respect for his character, and that the Clerk of this Court furnish a copy of this report to his family.

E. A. Nisbet,
W. Poe,
W. K. DeGraffenried,
Clifford Anderson,
Barney Hill.
Committee.

Judge Cole said:

Gentlemen: I fully endorse the eloquent and

merited resolutions just read, and unite with the Bar in rendering this just tribute to the memory of the late Gov. Cobb; and nowhere, in my opinion, can such a tribute more properly be paid to the memory of our departed brother than here, where the prominent talents and acquirements by which he adorned our profession have been so often and so lately displayed.

In the death of Gen. Cobb the Bar of Macon has lost one of its very brightest ornaments, and this Court one of its very ablest and most enlightened counselors. The State at large has sustained a severe loss in the death of this great and good man. His genius, his learning and his virtues have conferred an imperishable glory on his native State, whose liberties he fought to secure and whose institutions he labored to perpetuate. He was a patriot and statesman of spotless integrity and consummate wisdom.

But above all, he was the ornament of society, the genial and social friend and companion of every member of this Bar.

I have felt the death of Gov. Cobb very deeply. He was endeared to me by many ties. He was always kind and considerate, always indulgent and charitable to my many errors and shortcomings; and in all my intercourse with him here I ever found him a true and sincere Christian friend and gentleman.

Remarks of Hon. Washington Poe.

May it please your Honor: In rising to second the resolutions just offered, were I to be governed by the dictates of my judgment, I should not attempt to add one word to the appropriate, just and almost exhausting preamble submitted by the honorable chairman of the committee; but when I look upon that vacant chair and that unoccupied desk, and remember that he who so recently possessed them had granted me a measure of his friendship, my heart presents its claims, and I am induced to say a word or two, if only to serve as a means of laying my tribute of respect and affection on the honored tomb of our departed brother.

Although the preamble has been so extensive in its range, and has grouped together almost every element composing the noble character of our friend, yet there is one characteristic—and that an important one—which has been omitted. The preamble informs us that in the opening of the professional career of Gov. Cobb he was appointed Solicitor-General of his Judicial Circuit, and that very soon thereafter he became the Representative of his District in the Congress of the United States, and from the floor was elevated to the Speaker's chair of that august body, where he presided with credit to himself and almost unparalleled acceptance to his fellow-citizens. His next elevation was to the Executive chair of his native State, and then to a prominent place in the Cabinet of President Buchanan. With all these honors resting upon him, after being the peer and counselor of the last of the statesmen, he retires into private life and engages in the practice of the law, totally devoid of all pretence or presumption, and demeaning himself with the modesty of the most unofficial member in our midst, and requiring only truth and integrity as the guarantee of his friendship and confidence. Sir, I consider this trait in the character of Gov. Cobb as one of the brightest jewels in the crown of his earthly glory. But in view of all this success and renown, may not instruction, if not admonition, be deduced from it? We, my brethren of the Bar, are now ardently engaged in the duties of our laborious profession—some for wealth, some for honor, some for office, and some for fame; but let us remember and be admonished by this striking example that all

> "Await alike the inevitable hour;
> The paths of glory lead but to the grave."

What a long line of this brotherhood has passed the dark river before us! and we are rapidly following in their footsteps. There are Lumpkin, and McDonald, and Strong, and King, and the Tracys, and *our Cobb*, whose friendship and sweet converse we have so often enjoyed.

> "Around us each dissevered chain
> In shining ruin lies,
> And human hands can ne'er again
> Unite those broken ties."

Our departed brother left his home, with a part of his family, apparently in health, on a visit to the great commercial metropolis of this great and almost boundless country, and whilst in New York, and in the very midst of social intercourse, his last summons came to leave this world, with all its cares, anxieties and engagements. By the aid of that profound wisdom with which he was so largely endowed, he was not found unprepared for this great and final trial; but with perfect resignation to the call, and as one tired with the labors of the day disrobes himself for a night's repose, he calmly laid off his earthly habiliments, being fully convinced that there was prepared for him a robe of righteousness at God's right hand, and which all shall receive who, like him, in humility and faith, accept the imputed righteousness of Another. I second the resolutions.

Remarks of Samuel Hall, Esq.

May it please your Honor: While I do not arrogate to myself the ability "to paint the lily or gild refined gold," my feelings prompt me to lay an humble offering upon the tomb of one of the wisest and best men it has been my fortune to know—

> "Friend of man and friend of truth,
> The hope of age and guide of youth;
> Few hands like his, with virtue warmed,
> Few heads with knowledge so informed"—

to hold up his example to the younger members of the profession which he loved and adorned; to invite them to tread the path which led him to honor, usefulness and distinction; and to contemplate his illustrious career, and

> "Gaze upon the great
> Where neither guilty glory shines,
> Nor despicable stab."

From his earliest manhood Gov. Cobb was marked for distinction: his elevation to the high places of the Republic was almost simultaneous with his entry into public life. At thirty years of age he was Speaker of the popular branch of Congress—a position that had before been occupied by Stevenson, Polk, Hunter, Macon and other distinguished statesmen, but none of them discharged its duties with more signal ability than our departed friend. While he was Speaker I visited Washington City, and in company with a friend paid my respects to Mr. Clay, who asked me if I had been to the House of Representatives, and added that as a Georgian I would feel my pride glow upon contemplating the brilliant career of my fellow-countryman, (the Speaker), who had shed more dignity and lustre upon that station than any one since the days of Judge Cheves of South Carolina. He successively filled, with honor and usefulness, the Executive chair of this State, and the office of Secretary of the Treasury during most of the administration of the late President Buchanan. Yet, although his career as a statesman was immensely successful, he deeply regretted that more of his time had not been devoted to the study of his profession, and that he had not engaged more extensively in its practice. Men are not lawyers by intuition, and can only become so by long and assiduous study; but with an accurate knowledge of the general principles of the science, a mind like his could easily make the details from which these conclusions were deduced. Show him the magazine, and he would select the weapon the occasion required and wield it with a giant's strength and a master's skill. What seemed to cost him little effort was only to be obtained by persons less gifted after laborious application and painful vigils. This spot is suggestive of instances of the truth of this remark. In an interesting case that occurred during the present year, the principles involved had been discussed by one of the most gifted advocates of the State with an ability and copiousness that seemed to exhaust the subject; all appeared to think that nothing was left for Gov. Cobb to say, but in this anticipation they were mistaken. His clear discrimination, powerful analysis, sound judgment and unsurpassed powers of reasoning presented the cause in an entirely new and original light, and caused all to feel, as Justice Buller said *he* did upon listening to the luminous judgments of Lord Mansfield, that "his mind was lost in admiration at the stretch and strength of the human understanding."

Again, I have seen him victor over the combined legal talent of the State, and I hope I do no injustice to the just claims of the distinguished judges who presided in the case involving the constitutionality of the Stay Law of 1866, when I declare it as my conviction that most of their inspiration and reasoning was derived from his truly great argument on that occasion. His line of thought was singularly coincident with that of the Supreme Court of the United States when treating lately the same subject; he had never seen the case referred to, nor had the judges of that Court the benefit of his masterly argument and sound constitutional views.

His return to the Bar after the close of the war may, without much violence to language, be said to have been the commencement of his professional life in earnest. The vocation was highly agreeable to him, and he sought by every means in his power to elevate its character and augment its usefulness. He pursued it with ardor and enthusiasm, and made the thoughts of its great masters a part of his own intellectual and professional being. Justice as administered by the courts he ever regarded as the safeguard of society and the highest interest of the State: it was this that kept the body politic in harmony; "the highest was not exempt from its requirements," and "the least felt its care." Very foreign from his nature was everything like indirection. His mind instinctively repelled all finesse and sophistry. He sought truth, and when he found it he gave it the homage of his great and pure heart. From the constant and trying labors of his profession he found time to look after the educational and benevolent interests of the community. Few are aware of the extent of his benefactions, not only in the way of alms, but of kind offices and valuable advice. He boasted not himself of these deeds—he blew no trumpet before him—his right hand knew not what his left hand did;

"He did good by stealth, and blushed to own it fame."

All ages, sexes and conditions, who enjoyed the privilege of his acquaintance, felt an affectionate attachment to him. Not only the refined and enlightened citizens of the city, but the simple dwelling in remote hamlets, upon the announcement of his sudden death felt a sense of the great bereavement the country had sustained. The very children mourned him as they would a lost father. His coming always made them glad, and they witnessed his departure with feelings of regret—often with tears. He needs no monument to perpetuate his fame; his life is his monument; his cenotaph is in the hearts of his countrymen. The plaudits of his contemporaries will be caught up and prolonged by future generations, and will swell in volume and earnestness so long as virtue has a worshiper, as genius is admired, and true chivalry and nobleness of character are appreciated.

His mind was as broad as the universe, and he could not give up to sect or party what his Maker meant for mankind. He could not be contracted into the narrow confines of the intolerant and bigoted; his commerce was with the world, and it was impossible to dwarf him to the dimensions of a haberdasher of small wares. On the day previous to his death I received from him a letter communicating his improved health, and saying that he would meet me at his home on the fifteenth day of the month. But the enjoyment we anticipated from again taking him by the hand, listening to his wise conversation and hearing his lively sallies, was destined never to be realized; the places which once knew him were destined henceforth to know him no more for ever.

He was indeed brought home to rest in the bosom of a mother who had cherished him, and who, in his turn, he had honored by making her name loved and respected in every civilized country on the globe. He was laid by the side of those who were kindred spirits in life—Lumpkin, Dougherty, Deloney, and his own illustrious brother, Gen. Thos. R. R. Cobb. The mouldering ruins surrounding the mausoleum of the mighty dead are emblematic of their earthly career, while the beautiful Oconee, which flows hard by their last earthly resting-place and sings their perpetual requiem, now smiling in the sunshine, now stricken by the storm, will murmur on a thousand years and flow as it now flows, is typical of their better and immortal part. The summons, though sudden, did not find Gen. Cobb unprepared; in the very act of professing his Lord and Master to one of His chosen ambassadors, he was caught up and translated to the bosom of his Father and his God; and the angels in heaven, we doubt not, were in full sympathy with the ecstasies of those who had gone before at re-uniting with the loved one from whom they had been separated by the narrow boundaries between time and eternity. All that is left us now is to cherish his memory and follow his example—to emulate his virtues, and make timely preparation for the great ordeal which he has triumphantly passed, so that when the dread messenger comes, we too may be prepared to receive him, and go not hence like "a galley slave scourged to his dungeon," but sustained and soothed by an unfaltering trust—

> "Like one who wraps the drapery of his couch about him,
> And lies down to pleasant dreams."

Remarks by A. O. Bacon, Esq.

May it please your Honor: When a great man like Gen. Cobb dies, it is most fit that the tributes which are due to his character and worth should be paid by those who have been his contemporaries during the greater portion of his life; but there are some phases of his character which can be more properly spoken of by a young man; and in rising to do so I but obey the earnest promptings of my heart. Although it was my mournful privilege to see him laid in the grave, it is difficult for me to realize that Gen. Cobb is dead. Such a very short time ago he was with us and of us, in outward appearance the picture of robust health, the idol of his family, the pride of his friends and the life and soul of the social circle; and now that we say he is no more, it is difficult to realize that so much of life is indeed dead; that his eye, so beaming with liveliest emotions of love and sympathy, has for ever lost its lustre; that his voice, whose thrilling tones of eloquence we have so often listened to in this chamber, and which was ever ready to enliven, assist and direct, has been hushed in death; and that his hand, lately so warm in friendship's clasp, is now but cold and lifeless clay. To me, as to the other members of this Bar, Gen. Cobb's loss is a personal affliction. Through a period of twelve years, by unnumbered kindnesses, he taught me to know him as my friend, and unconsciously I grew to love him better than a friend. And what I say here will be endorsed by all the young men who were so fortunate as to enjoy his acquaintance. He was truly the young man's friend. He possessed eminently the faculty of endearing himself to young men with whom he came in contact. This was not owing to effort upon his part with a design to increase his popularity, but his large, warm and peculiarly sympathetic heart naturally led him to understand and appreciate the many difficulties and trials which young men encounter in the beginning of life, especially in the beginning of professional life.

These he was ever ready to assist with counsel, encouragement and advice, and also with pecuniary aid if needed. With these kind offices, in the performance of which he never wearied, he "grappled them to his soul with hooks of steel." Not only so, for this man of mature age, giant intellect and vast experience, who had "sounded all the depths of greatness," was not only the faithful friend, but also the genial, familiar companion, to the young man inexperienced, and, compared with him, of little knowledge. In the hearts of thousands of young men all over this land he has raised "a monument more lasting than brass;" and when this and the next generation shall have followed him to the grave, the story of his excellent worth will, in the lessons of the fireside, be told to our children's children.

Allusions have been made, in the report of the committee, to the happiness of his family relations. This is sacred ground, upon which we may not intrude too far or tread too lightly. But to those of us who were permitted to see the beauty of those relations its memory will never fade. His faith in the virtue and purity of woman, and his knightly respect and veneration for her person and character, bore their legitimate fruits in his devotion and tenderness to his wife and daughters. To his grown sons he was at once the devoted father and genial companion. In the company of his little children, his great heart overflowed with genuine happiness, and among them he was again a child, even the most boisterous and gleeful.

In the virtue of hospitality he was pre-eminent—not from policy, not for the gratification of pride in the display of wealth, but with his big, generous nature—the most generous I ever knew—he loved to have his friends around him and share with them the best he had. His house was ever open to the friend and the stranger, and amid the bounteous profusion which ever covered his generous board, the chiefest pleasures which the guest experienced were the freedom and sincerity of the genial hospitality which he dispensed. About Gen. Cobb there was nothing small; he was great in all things. His nature was open, frank, generous, hilarious, enthusiastic, affectionate, tender, sympathetic, sincere. Add to this a peerless intellect, a brilliant wit which never hesitated, failed or carelessly wounded, joined to a happy address which ever found its way by the shortest route to every heart, and we have a faint outline of this splendid, magnificent man. As a lawyer, the report of the committee has assigned him to his appropriate position in the front rank of the profession. In the field of oratory he was indeed regal. He swept with master hand all the chords of human passion, and the strains of his eloquence fell upon and enveloped his hearers as with the weird spell of an incantation. Truly, "upon his lips had the mystic bee dropped the honey of persuasion."

But he has gone! How painful that our heart-strings should be so violently torn from the object of our love! How terrible that this grand man, towering in his strength, should so suddenly fall powerless and lifeless before the unexpected stroke of death! It is sad to see the decayed and lifeless trunk, swaying its bare and leafless arms in the blast, fall before the fury of the storm. But when we see some great oak, a giant among its fellows, its huge arms and thick foliage indicating its strength and vigor, its green leaves but tinged with the hues of coming autumn—when we see this pride of the forest, when all is calm and still, when no breeze ruffles its foliage—fall with a resounding crash to the earth, we are struck dumb with awe.

General Cobb occupied so much space in men's hearts and before the public eye that his sudden taking away can but leave a great void. We are all painfully conscious that this void cannot be satisfactorily filled by another. Only himself could do it. The devoted, tender husband and father, the fast, unfailing friend, the generous and genial companion, the hospitable and benevolent citizen, the brilliant orator, the great statesman, has gone from among us, and we never shall see his like again.

Remarks of Judge James Jackson.

May it please your Honor: If the spirits of the departed are permitted to revisit the scenes of earth, and to be cognizant of what happens here, then is the spirit of my beloved kinsman, friend and partner, gratified to-day. The great respect which he felt for your Honor, as the presiding officer of this court and as a man, I know full well; the profound esteem in which he held the venerable and distinguished gentleman who prepared and offered the preamble and resolutions, and the no less venerable and honorable gentleman who seconded the resolutions, is equally known to me; I know, too, the closer tie of long personal friendship and kindly sympathy which bound him to the able and learned gentleman from Fort Valley, and the almost paternal affection with which he regarded my younger brother, whose feeling tribute to his memory is yet ringing in our ears; I know the cordial kindness which he felt toward every member of this bar; therefore, may it please your Honor, I know that no tribute of respect to his memory, not even that which bathed all Athens, the scene of his boyhood and lifelong friendships, in tears over his bier, could gratify him more than this testimonial from this Bench and this Bar.

May it please your Honor: General Cobb had within him much of the "*esprit de corps*"—the love of the profession—of the brotherhood—of the family of lawyers. Whenever and wherever he saw a lawyer—especially a young lawyer—struggling under adverse circumstances, he felt like throwing his own great arm around him and lifting him up. Hence the Bar of the Western Circuit—the younger members of it particularly—ever gathered around and leaned upon him; and hence this Bar with whom he had mingled but three years—all of them, from the oldest to the youngest—respected, may I not say loved him living, and now gather to-day to participate, not coldly and formally, but from their hearts and with deep feeling, in honoring him dead!

May it please your Honor: Whether present in spirit or not, my beloved partner is not visibly present to express gratification and return thanks; but surely if any living man may personate the dead and speak in his behalf, then of all men living I have the right and mine is the duty to speak in the name of Howell Cobb.

Sir, when I was a boy, my father, embarrassed by pecuniary difficulties, was forced to sell his residence in Athens and remove to the country; and from that time the house of Colonel John A. Cobb, the father of Howell Cobb, became my home during my scholastic course. Howell Cobb was some four years my senior, yet the room in the house familiarly known even to the servants as the boys' room, he and myself occupied together; and though the old mansion itself has long since been torn down and its site is now in the possession of strangers, that room is still vividly before me, with the bed in which he lay and that which I occupied; and, may it please your Honor, though but a boy, he gave to me his confidence then, and through the long series of years which have followed he never withdrew it. When but a boy I leaned upon him, because he was stronger, physically, mentally and morally, than I was, and when the news came of his death, I felt myself leaning upon him still. I loved him—may it please your Honor, I loved him more than I loved any man. I loved him, and watched his brilliant career with a satisfaction equal to that which would have inspired me had my own ambition been borne on the same triumphant tide.

But it is not my purpose to speak of the great powers of his intellect; it is not my purpose to trace his career as a statesman, who, elected to Congress at the age of twenty-six, became at thirty the foremost man in the House of Representatives and leader of the Polk administration party in that House; nor is it my purpose to portray him as Speaker of that House, presiding with such promptness, efficiency and dignity as to draw those plaudits from Henry Clay of which my brother has just spoken; nor shall I speak of him as Governor of Georgia, nor as Secretary of the Treasury of the United States, nor as the President of the Provisional Congress which assembled at Montgomery and Richmond; nor shall I speak of his sacrifices and services, civic and military, to that which must now go down in history as the "Lost Cause;" nor shall I address this Bench and Bar in respect to his vast powers as lawyer and advocate displayed here under your Honor's eye, in other Circuits, and before the Supreme Court of Georgia.

No, sir—of none of these will I speak; these are known and read of all men; but they describe not the man whom I loved so much and so long. "'Tis the soul that makes the man." Of the soul of Howell Cobb—of the inner man—of that spark of divinity which comes down from heaven, and kindling clay into life makes that life like God's—of the seat of the emotions, the source of the affections—of that whence everything noble, pure and good flows to nourish, vivify and beautify humanity—of this innate principle within the breast of Howell Cobb, exemplified by the outward deeds of a lifetime, of this and these I will speak to your Honor, for a moment.

Sir, *his was the soul of melting charity;* and the Divine spark was all aglow within him in this the noblest and best of human qualities—the beginning, the end, the sum of Christian graces. He was the most charitable man I have ever known. Not a ragged urchin in this, or any other community ever asked him for alms and went off denied; not one widow or other suffering child of humanity ever approached Howell Cobb for aid without finding in him a friend and a brother. His charity always, too, proceeded from the great Bible principle of love—love to the common brotherhood of man. "If a man love not his brother whom he has seen, how shall he love God whom he has not seen?"

Sir, I believe that the man whose soul I am trying to photograph was under the dominion of the grace of Christ long before he knew and fully recognized God in Christ. His charity ever took a religious turn. Ministers of the Cross were ever its most favored objects.

I remember asking him years ago, on returning from Franklin Court, what he had charged the Rev. Wm. J. Parks for services rendered in an important and hotly-litigated lawsuit in that county; his reply is as fresh in my mind as if given yesterday: "Do you suppose, Judge, that I would exchange for any amount of money the prayers of such a man as Mr. Parks, for me and for my family?"

Nor did he do anything by halves. He was whole-hearted—his liberality exhaustless, or only exhausted when purse was empty and credit gone. I remember to have been told by the Rev. Mr. Warren, the Baptist minister of this city, that soon after the close of the war he received a note from Mrs. Cobb, in behalf of her husband and herself, begging him to accept an accompanying donation. Mrs. Cobb was not then a member of Mr. Warren's congregation, her church membership being in Athens, but she had enjoyed the benefit of his ministry at intervals of temporary sojourn in Macon, during the war. He opened the enclosure, and found that it contained a greenback note for $500.

Another incident occurs to my mind. During the last year or two of the war, continuous streams of Confederate troops swept daily by the residence of Bishop Pierce in Hancock county. The latch was ever on the outside of the Bishop's door; his house and smoke-house were opened wide to the wants of the suffering soldiery, until all his supplies were swept away, and himself and family left with nothing. My father-in-law, Mr. Mitchell, conveyed the information to General Cobb, who straightway sent from his plantation wagon-loads of bacon and stores to supply the deficiency in the Bishop's larder.

At the close of the war, he called upon the Rev. Wm. Flinn of the Presbyterian church at Milledgeville, and insisted upon knowing his pecuniary condition, and how he managed to support his family and himself—stating that he knew that his parishoners must be poor from the effects of the war, and unable to do much for him. Mr. Flinn told me that he tried to put him off, but General Cobb insisted on his right to know and relieve his wants, extorted from him his condition, and sent him ample supplies for himself and household for a twelvemonth.

I remember once telling him that the Rev. Allen Turner, a very holy but very peculiar servant of God, had imbibed the opinion of him entertained by many who did not or would not know him, that he was irreligious, dissipated and profane; that I had tried to disabuse Mr. Turner of the idea, but feared that I had failed. I was on a visit to his house at the time, and the conversation occurred in the sitting-room in the presence of others. Before I left he took me aside into a private room, handed me a twenty-dollar greenback, and said, "Will you hand this to Mr. Turner, and without telling who sent it, say to him that a man who hopes he is not so bad a man as he thinks him, gives that to an old, worn-out servant of God. I do not think he is to be blamed," he added, "for entertaining opinions of me which others, who ought to know better, have circulated far and wide."

To the Rev. Josephus Anderson of the Florida Conference—a gentleman whose acquaintance he made whilst stationed at Quincy during the war, and whom he much admired and loved—he sent suits of clothing, and to the wife of that gentleman dresses in keeping with the presents to her husband.

Whilst at his funeral at Athens, I learned from a gentleman who derived his information from the merchant himself, that during the current year he had given orders to the amount of one thousand dollars for provisions furnished to the widows and orphans of Athens and its vicinity, and I heard that some poor widow there had, since his death, weepingly acknowledged the receipt of fifty dollars in money from him.

But, may it please your Honor, I may not recount half the deeds of his charitable soul which I myself know. And these deeds, for the most part, have come to my knowledge since his decease. Here, too, the spark divine had lighted his soul: "When thou doest thine alms, let not thy left hand know what thy right hand doeth." He died, and the lifelong friend of his bosom was not aware of the tithe of his good deeds, though that friend had thought that he breathed into his ear almost every secret of his soul.

His was the soul of hospitality. And herein, too, the spark divine caught upon material that lighted his whole man into a flame. The commandment of the Apostle was in full harmony with the boundings of his own big heart. He was the most liberal-hearted, the most widely hospitable man I have ever known. His house was stretched to embrace all. I have known—I think I speak within the bounds of truth—of fifty persons lodging and eating with him at his Macon home at one time. At Athens, at Washington, at Milledgeville, wherever he lived, he was the same—his house ever full, yet, like an omnibus, never so full as not to take others in.

His was the soul of honor. And surely, sir, if integrity and truth be the corner-stones of honor, herein too is the divine illumination apparent; for Jesus, the man-God, is not only the Way and the Life, but the Truth; and sin, in its last analysis, is but a denial and rejection of the truth of God.

Once, when Speaker, his honor, in connection with the journal of the House, was called in question by Mr. Preston King of New York.

Gen. Cobb instantly vacated the chair and called to it his Whig competitor, Mr. Winthrop of Massachusetts, whom he had defeated for the position. The result was his unanimous acquittal by the committee named by Mr. Winthrop, and the unanimous endorsement of their report by the House.

In his young manhood, his father, by requesting his endorsement, involved him in debt to the amount of seventy thousand dollars. By using a clause in his uncle's will which, he was advised, gave him most of the large property of his father on his attaining twenty-one years of age, he could have applied that property to the extinguishment of the liabilities he had endorsed, and left unendorsed creditors to whistle for their money. But the high tone of his unselfish honor would not permit him to use the means. He felt that his father had been credited upon the strength of that large property as his own, and rather than see his good name reproached my noble kinsman, may it please your Honor, labored for twenty years under the burden of this security debt, the last item of which was only paid about the beginning of our civil war.

When Governor of Georgia, he made three trips to the North to sell her bonds. Mr. Mitchell, the Treasurer of the State, insisted that he should pay his expenses out of the contingent fund, citing precedent after precedent of others who had occupied the Executive chair; but he replied,

"No; Georgia pays me three thousand dollars as

my salary for all my services; I have no right to touch a dollar more of her money."

His was the soul of true, unalterable, constant friendship; and herein, too, it resembled the soul of Him who "sticketh closer than a brother"—who, "having loved his own, loved them to the end." He was a true man, may it please your Honor—true to the cause he espoused, true to the friend he loved. However others may have shifted their course in that great struggle "which tried men's souls" indeed, and which resulted so disastrously to Southern interests, having fixed his eye in the beginning upon the Polar star, there its gaze remained riveted to the end. The cause, the cause, everything for the cause! was his inspiring cry from the first to the last of that mighty contest. And, sir, while the chain was, as it were, around his own limbs, when he heard that Mr. Secretary Seward had tauntingly said that no human being at the South had asked for the release of Mr. Davis from Fortress Monroe, Gen. Cobb wrote Mr. Seward from Athens to the effect that every man at the South, who had manhood in him, felt equally guilty with our illustrious but ill-fated chief—that every true heart bled for his sufferings, and that the only reason why the universal wail was not heard at Washington was the fear that its cry might do harm rather than good to the representative of our common "Lost Cause."

And when at last the illustrious prisoner was admitted to bail, Gen. Cobb tendered to him and his family a home in his household, or, if he preferred it, the free use of either of his residences—that at Macon, at Athens or at Americus. This, sir, I know to be a fact, from personal knowledge.

Sir, if my partner died with unkind feelings in his bosom toward a human being that God had made, it was feeling engendered by wrong done, as he thought, to a friend whom he loved, and who had reciprocated that love to the hour of his death; and when the grave closed over that friend, he seemed to have felt that friendship for the dead required him to inherit the wrong and pursue and punish the wrong-doer.

May it please your Honor, this fidelity to friendship is the reason why Howell Cobb had friends such as few men ever possessed. His friends loved him because he loved them; not for his great intellect, for Satan's capacity equals perhaps that of the archangel, yet who loves Satan? It was the fellowship of Howell Cobb with men and his love for man which made men love him.

Love begets love. This is the principle which underlies all affection in all the relations of life. Husband and wife, parents and children, brothers and sisters are all tied together by this cord of mutual love; nay, more, sir, this is the corner-stone of our holy religion: "we love Christ because he first loved us." So the friends of my friend loved him because he loved them, and proved that love in a thousand ways.

Sir, I stand before you a living illustration of his friendship on the one hand, and, all I had to give him in return, my love, on the other. I read law in his office, and as soon as I was admitted he took me in as a partner, and insisted on sharing with me the salary as well as the perquisites of the office of Solicitor-General which he then held. I have now in my possession letters from him, authorizing me to draw without limit on his factors during his absence. He knew my pecuniary condition, and gave them to me in full confidence that I would not abuse it. On their authority I could have drawn all he had in that house.

Sir, his friendship for me, manifested so often

and so long, was strikingly exhibited at Athens in August last. We had been retained in a cause which involved a very large property, and were entitled, he thought, to a fee of five thousand dollars. He said to me that the war had left me without property—without even a home—and urged me, on my return to Macon, to collect that fee and purchase a homestead. I said to him that I would be left too much behind on our books. He replied that he did not wish it to appear at all upon the books, nor did he wish any note of it made. If I should ever be able to repay him, well; if not, he could make no investment of twenty-five hundred dollars which would gratify him more than in the purchase of a home for me and my little orphans. The fee was not collected, nor the purchase made; but with me, sir, the will was the deed; and the noble heart and abiding friendship of my generous kinsman are as fully illustrated in the one as they would have been in the other.

May it please your Honor, had I not loved such a man; had I not been willing to make any sacrifice consistent with honor to serve him, I should have been less than man; and the wonder how or why his friends so loved and adhered to him ceases the moment those friends reveal to mankind the secret throbbings of that heart, now, alas! pulseless for ever!

How much I did love this man! How much respect him! How I wept over his grave! I know nothing, may it please your Honor, to which I can liken my love for him save that which Jonathan bore to David; and had I, like Jonathan, been the heir of Israel's throne, I would have placed the crown on his brow as nobler, purer, worthier than my own!

His was the soul of kindness and mercy to all inferiors and dependants; and oh! if there be one link that binds the Saviour stronger and closer to our hearts than all others, it is his loving-kindness and tender mercy toward us so inferior to, so helplessly dependent upon, him!

Sir, in the time of slavery no lash was ever applied by him to the back of a slave, nor would he tolerate in employe or overseer the slightest touch of inhumanity to his slaves. I do not remember in the close intimacy of a lifetime to have heard him use a harsh expression or to have seen him cast an angry glance toward the servants about him. His was ever the law of love, and so he ruled household and dependants with talismanic power. Wherever he sojourned he was a favorite with all servants. His was the first buggy and horse brought to the door when Court broke and lawyers left, and great was the contest among ostlers upon whom should devolve the task of attending to Mars. Howell's horse. His room was the first to be served—water brought—fire made—wood and lightwood furnished in abundance—because his was the gentlest voice, the kindest look, the most liberal hand.

May it please your Honor, should the eye of the little pages at Washington when he was member and Speaker, rest upon these remarks in print, they, though grown to manhood now, will recognize the identity of this feature of the great, good soul of Howell Cobb; for toward them was ever the same voice and look and hand.

This trait of his character was ever strikingly manifested toward children. In the summer of 1867, in the absence of his family at Athens, he spent much of his time at my house, and every little heart among my little ones beat quicker and each eye sparkled brighter at his approach; for all knew that candy or sugar-plum or toy ever followed in his wake. His big, paternal heart embraced all the young, the guileless, the innocent, and rejoiced to see them happy.

Sir, He who said, "Suffer little children to come unto me and forbid them not"—He who embraced them in his own Divine arms, had taken something of his own blessed spirit and mingled it with the spirit of Howell Cobb.

His was the soul of the reverential son, the indulgent, loving, ever-forgiving father, the perfectly single-hearted and ever-devoted husband. Surely, sir, He who was "obedient to his Father unto death—even the death of the cross;" He who was, is and ever will be the most indulgent, loving, long-suffering, forgiving of all Fathers; He who as husband loves, cherishes, nurses with sleepless vigilance night and day—wearing her image ever on his own divine heart—his bride, the Church of God; surely, sir, He had herein, too, touched long ago, with his grace, the heart of Howell Cobb, and made it kindred to his own.

I never knew a more reverential son. An affront to himself was comparatively nothing—the slightest shadow of disrespect to his father aroused all the lion within him. A distinguished gentleman, pronouncing an eulogium upon the character of his brother, Gen. T. R. R. Cobb, attributed the greatness of that gentleman in intellectual and moral power in a great degree to the influence and training of his father-in-law, Judge Lumpkin. Gen. Cobb lived, perhaps, to forgive, but he never forgot the remark. He considered it insulting to the memory of his own noble, venerable and venerated father, whom he considered the equal of any man in great practical common sense and judgment, and inferior to none in all those moral and religious attributes which make the man and fit him to impress manhood upon those whom he rears at the fireside.

I shall not trust myself, sir, to speak of his tenderness to his mother. She was the best of women, and from her heart, overflowing with love for all around her, her son of whom I now speak drew much of the inspiration of his own noble soul. Her memory is as dear to me, sir, almost as that of my own mother, for her voice was always gentle and her look ever the glance of love to the boy that sat at her fireside and ate at her table.

What a father was this noble man! How by the hour has he unbosomed himself to me about his children—revealed his hopes and his fears—

felicitated himself on the happy marriages of his three grown sons, and talked as lovingly of their wives as if sprung from his own loins! How solicitous about *the souls* of his children long before he felt assured that his own was safe! How often has he told me that he would not for worlds have one of them suspect that he doubted the divinity of Jesus! So that alone, at his own fireside, he bore in his breast the secret that agonized his doubting, struggling heart so long. He would not reveal it to her whom he loved better than his soul, for he knew how it would grieve her Christian heart; and to shield her from every pang was the absorbing care of his domestic life!

What a grandfather was he! I see him now at his Athens home, with three or four of these little ones prattling around him—heedful of all their little wants—joyful in all their innocent prattle—happier, far happier, than when pomp and place and power were at his nod. Often when summoned to Macon on business, in Summer and Fall has he expressed to me his exquisite enjoyment of their innocent gambols, and how he longed to be with those little ones again!

May it please your Honor, even I, twin-brother

in affection to the dead, may not unveil more of the curtain of his happy home-life. I may not speak of him in reference to her, the one object of his love through life. I know all its single-eyed devotion—its inception—its constant growth—its beautiful, ripe, mellow fullness in autumnal life. When he was courting her, boy though I was, he confided in me, told me his hopes and fears, his alternations of courage and doubt, and revealed to me, sooner perhaps than to any one else, his success and engagement.

I have witnessed the flush of pride on his face by her side in the splendors of Washington society. I have seen the unutterable agony of that face when she lay on the bed of sickness which he feared might be the bed of death! True to every cause he ever espoused; true to every friend who ever served him; this man, who was indeed a man in the full stature of moral manhood, was true in every fibre of his big soul to the woman who gave him her young heart and who almost worshiped him through life! He respected her intellectual and moral nature as much as he loved her; and often, very often, has he told me that he would give the universe, if he held it in his hand, to possess the simple faith and trust in Christ which he saw daily exhibited and exemplified in her home-life.

Blessed be God! that faith in Christ was at last the reward of a long struggle to obtain it, and his soul became a soul redeemed—regenerated and "born again" by the grace of our Lord Jesus Christ. Yes, sir; above all and better than all I have yet said, *his was the soul of "a child of God," full born, with unmistakable features of Divine paternity!*

Sir, it is a source of infinite satisfaction to feel that whilst he knew me to be but a poor, frail, weak, sinful, erring man, he had confidence in my integrity as a Christian. I have the great satisfaction of knowing that immediately on our coming to Macon to practice law, before my family had removed here from Milledgeville, or his from Athens, whilst we occupied his house alone, he opened his heart to me on the great subject of religion. The conversation occurred on the stoop of his house on Walnut street, and from that moment I felt that the Spirit of the Most High was leading him, and that that Spirit would "lead him into all truth." He spoke of his aged father and his sisters and brothers, all of whom had been members of some Christian church, and himself, the eldest born, still out. He spoke of the overwhelming impression made upon him at a communion service in the church of the Rev. Mr. Anderson, at Quincy, when his brother, Major John B. Cobb, and others of his staff left their places at his side to kneel at that solemn service. His thoughts ascended to the marriage supper of the Lamb, in heaven; to his venerable father, deceased several years before, and who dying had laid his hands on his head and, blessing him, had said, "Howell, my son, meet me in heaven;" to his pious brother, Gen. T. R. R. Cobb, who had recently fallen on the battle-field of Fredericksburg, in sight of the house where their mother was born; and the thought fell upon his mind with crushing force, *Shall I be separated for ever from these?*

Sir, whilst he thus talked to me every lineament of his marked face heaved, and tears fell like rain from his eyes. I told him that he ought to unite with the Church of Christ at once. He replied that he would gladly do so if there was one that would take him in, but that he could not comprehend that God ever was in man—that he doubted the divinity of Christ, and he could not and would not join any Church with a lie on his lips.

May it please your Honor, is it wonderful that any mind should pause at the threshold of the stupendous thought that the infinite and self-existing Creator of all should condescend to become a man—a humble, despised and rejected man—a buffeted, persecuted and crucified man? "Great is the mystery of godliness!" exclaimed the Apostle of the Gentiles, as he grasped the thought of God in the humanity of Christ—a mystery only capable of solution by simple, child-like faith. The manner in which Gen. Cobb was led to imbibe the great truth, and hold and press it to his heart, adds another to the many instances of the wonderful providences of the Almighty.

Mr. William Hope Hull in the month of June last paid him a visit by appointment. Gen. Cobb's family were in Athens for the summer, and himself away for a day or two by an unexpected call. He requested me to entertain Mr. Hull until his return. I had known Mr. Hull from boyhood. I knew that whilst he was then, and had been for years, a firm believer in the religion of Christ, he had once been skeptical. I knew that he had read largely on the subject—skeptical works and those upholding the truth as it is in Jesus; and the thought recurred to me that he might be of service to my friend on the great subject which so occupied his thoughts and so much perplexed his mind. Accordingly, I asked him if he had ever conversed with Gen. Cobb upon the subject of religion. He said he had not. I told him that it was, when not engaged in business, our constant topic, and that to Gen. Cobb it was the most interesting subject of conversation; and after telling him of the difficulties in the way of Gen. Cobb, I suggested to him to talk to him upon the subject—stating that on the General's return they would be together alone in his house, and would have every opportunity of free and full interchange of views. He replied that he thought he had in his mind a book which must satisfy any intelligent mind—especially such a mind as Gen. Cobb's—of the divinity of Jesus and the reality of the man-God; and if in town, he would buy it and present it to him. Shortly thereafter he returned to my office with "The Christ of History," which was the book referred to, and which he had found at the store of Mr. Burke. On Gen. Cobb's return, Mr. Hull gave him that book, and they conversed freely during Mr. Hull's stay upon the great theme.

A few days after Mr. Hull's departure, Gen. Cobb came into the office with brow unclouded, and a light in his eye and serenity about his face which I had not observed there for months—nay years, before—and said to me that "The Christ of History" was the greatest book, the most unanswerable argument, he had ever read; that it had removed all his doubts of the divinity of Christ; and that his mind was relieved from the apprehension of death and the uncertainty of the Hereafter. Sir, it becomes me not to say how much I rejoiced at the glad tidings. Suffice it to say, that on that day or the next I told the Rev. Mr. Warren that Gen. Cobb was converted. He immediately sought an interview at the General's house, and becoming perfectly satisfied of his true conversion, observed, as he was about to depart, that they should give thanks to God for the great change which he had experienced. They both fell upon their knees, and Mr. Warren subsequently stated to me he never heard a heartier Amen than that which came from the heart of Gen. Cobb. Both, he informed me, rose from their knees bathed in tears, and that good man, grasping both of Gen. Cobb's hands in his own, welcomed him into the fold of Christ.

Sir, at Athens in August, I saw him again, and was again struck with an unusual simplicity of manner and quietness of deportment; and having occasion to narrate to him an incident which in other days would have aroused the lion within him, I found the lion a lamb. The strong man had become a confiding child—a babe had been born for heaven.

Sir, at New York he died in the very act of confessing his Saviour to Bishop Beckwith of the Episcopal Church, and from that confession of Jesus upon earth before men, his spirit ascended to be confessed by Jesus before his Father and the angels, in heaven.

So, may it please your Honor, though sorrowing for my kinsman and my best and dearest friend, I "sorrow not as those without hope." I know as well as I know anything, that Him whom he had long and earnestly and anxiously sought he at last found. He had told me a hundred times that he was ready to give up every earthly aspiration and fruition for truth—truth in regard to God, to eternity; and no such man ever was, ever can be lost. I know that he loved honor, truth, purity, holiness, and that he loved these as impersonated in Jesus. I know that he loved Jesus, and, loving Him, loved most those who lived nearest to Him; and I know as well as I know anything which I cannot see that God, in great mercy, had prepared him for that great change which took place in the city of New York. This dispensation of Divine Providence was all arranged by that inscrutable, unsearchable Being "who doeth all things well."

Whilst it was his intention, often expressed to me, to unite with the Baptist Church—the Church through which his father and mother had ascended before him to glory, and the Church of the wife whom he loved so devotedly, yet my brother Hall is right. He was not, he could not have been, a sectarian. He would have ever loved your Honor—an Episcopalian; he would have loved these gentlemen—Presbyterians; he would have loved me and other Methodists; and he would have loved him most, to whatever branch of the Church of Christ he belonged, who approximated in character and conduct nearest to our great Lord and Head—our common exemplar—the Lord Jesus Christ.

I have thus sketched before your Honor the

outlines of the grand portrait I see before the eye of my mind. The sketch is imperfect, but, such as it is, it unveils a majestic soul—the soul of one who was indeed "A prince in Israel;" without exception the best man, the noblest specimen of our fallen humanity, it has ever been my fortune to know. I say not that the original was perfect, for there are spots even on the sun; but I do say that the rays of light emitted from all that was luminous and lovely about him so obscure every spot that even the eye of telescopic criticism cannot discern and locate one.

I have not transferred the picture in all its fullness to canvas, for it is beyond the power of the most skillful artist, even when the heart guides the hand, to paint the sun, and I possess no qualification of such an artist but the hand of affection. Even from this rude sketch, however, your Honor will see the nobility of his soul, and your own knowledge of the man, drawn from your intercourse with him, public and private, will enable you to fill much of the picture, and to complete in thought the work I must leave undone.

Friend of my boyhood, of my vernal summer, autumnal manhood, farewell, but not for ever!

Winter is rapidly whitening my own brow, and the blood courses more and more sluggishly through veins congealed with much of its snow and ice; contemporaries sink out of sight daily around me; all things admonish me "the time is short." Faith, simple, childlike, helpless, clinging faith, in that Jesus whom you, my friend, confessed with your dying lips—faith in that "house of many mansions" prepared by Him for all who confess, trust, love Him here—leads me confidently to anticipate the day when you and I shall sit down together in some quiet nook in that vast mansion of the redeemed, and talk over the struggles and conflicts, the trials and triumphs, the victories and defeats, the joys and sorrows which we encountered so long hand-in-hand here; and, smiling at the empty bubbles which so allured the ambition of our earthly hearts, we shall together adore that wonderful providence which through unseen and diverse paths, yet with unerring accuracy, brought us at last to rest, peace, joy, for ever!

And now, may it please your Honor, in the name of that widowed heart at Athens which will grieve for him so long as that heart is flesh; in the name of his children, whose hearts will glow at the mere mention of his name so long as those hearts shall beat; in the name of the little grandchildren whose innocent prattle he loved so much, and whose little arms would ever stretch out to meet him; in the name of his numerous relatives and many friends, all of whom loved him as only such a man can be loved; and in my own name, who loved him not less than most of these,—I return you and my brethren of the Bar thanks for this testimonial of affection and respect to HOWELL COBB.

ACTION OF THE SUPREME COURT OF GEORGIA.

At its session in August, 1869, at Atlanta, the Supreme Court of Georgia appointed a committee, consisting of Samuel Hall, Esq., chairman, E. A. Nisbet, William Ezzard, William Hope Hull, and Judge D. A. Vason, to take into consideration the death of Hon. Howell Cobb. On the morning of the 12th of August the committee made its report, which consisted of an adoption of the resolutions and sketch of General Cobb that had been prepared by Hon. E. A. Nisbet at the request of the Macon Bar, of which General Cobb was a member. The resolutions and sketch were adopted at the session of the Bibb Superior Court on the 30th of

November, 1869, and are printed in full in this volume. At the conclusion of the report to the Supreme Court, Chief-Justice Brown, from his seat on the Bench, delivered the following Address:

ADDRESS OF CHIEF-JUSTICE BROWN, OF THE SUPREME COURT OF GEORGIA.

Gentlemen of the Bar: In behalf of the Court, I submit the following reply to your report and resolutions:

General Howell Cobb was no ordinary man. His name will occupy a large space in the history of his country and the times in which he lived. Richly endowed by nature with intellectual strength, which had been developed and cultivated in a very high degree, he was eminently fitted for the many responsible positions which, by the free suffrage of his countrymen, he was called to fill. To great ability and force of character were added industry and energy, forming a combination which seldom fails to achieve success.

General Cobb was admitted to the Bar at an early age, as stated in your report, and commenced the active duties of life, as a lawyer, in the Western Circuit, in this, his native State. With the advantages of a fine personal appearance, a mind remarkably active, logical and penetrating, aided by a liberal education, he rose rapidly to position and distinction in his profession. But he was soon called by the people to lay aside, in a great measure, his professional pursuits, and to serve them, as he did during most of the remainder of his life, in high official positions of great importance and responsibility.

In the Congress of the United States, where he served during a long period of its proudest history, he not only won rank as a man, but he exercised great control as a leader.

In the Executive Chair of his State his administration was distinguished for ability, liberality and a vigilant attention to all the duties imposed upon him.

Of the course of General Cobb during the latter and more thrilling scenes through which we have passed I will not now speak. Justice requires that the history of these times, as it is to be transmitted to posterity, shall not be written, nor the motives and conduct of men who acted as prominent a part as did General Cobb to be too freely criticised, till the passions and prejudices which were engendered during the contest have entirely subsided, and Reason has resumed her sway. When posterity has seen results, the historian, with the materials which will be preserved and placed at his command, will be able to assign his proper position to each of the leading spirits who took part in the war and in the construction of the government after the disastrous and crushing defeat of the armies of the South and the hopeless loss of her cause.

During the high excitement of the past, and the great conflict of opinion as to what was the best that could be done for our almost ruined section, under all the circumstances by which they were surrounded at the close of the civil war, it was the misfortune of some of us to differ widely from General Cobb, and in the excitement of the times, when men had too little charity for each other while sitting in judgment upon motives, those differences may, in some cases, have been productive of personal alienation, which led to crimination and recrimination.

But all these differences, which grew out of conflicting opinions on public policy in times of high political excitement, and produced alienation and estrangement, are evanescent and soon pass away.

In the grave they are forgotten. And when, under Divine Providence, one party precedes the other, for a little while, to that habitation which awaits all the living, they are never remembered and cherished by any honorable and generous survivor.

General Cobb was not only an honorable, upright citizen in all the private walks of life, but he was distinguished for many noble traits of character and many private and social virtues. In his death Georgia has lost one of her ablest statesmen; the Bar, one of its brightest ornaments; society, one of its most cherished members, and his intelligent and amiable family, an affectionate, kind, indulgent husband and parent.

But relatives, friends and professional associates, as well as States and nations, must bow in submission to these afflictive dispensations of Providence, and we must all say reverently, "Thy will be done."

It affords the Court pleasure to testify their respect for the memory of General Cobb, as a distinguished member of this Bar, by directing that the preamble and resolutions be entered upon the minutes of this Court, in compliance with the request therein contained. And it is so ordered.

Action of the Board of Trustees of the University of Georgia, on the Announcement of the Death of General Howell Cobb.

Since our last regular meeting, Death has caused us, in common with his family, his friends, society and his country, to weep at the tomb of one of our most illustrious fellow-citizens, and one of our ablest, most devoted and earnest co-laborers in the great work of promoting art, science and education through the instrumentality of the University of Georgia.

Howell Cobb, an orator, statesman, patriot and Christian, is no more. His life was devoted to the service of his country, the maintenance of the rights and happiness of his fellow-citizens, to the cause of virtue and the pursuit of truth.

His education was begun and finished in the schools of this University. In its very threshold—at the grammar-school and University—he exhibited those moral, social and intellectual characteristics which won such confidence, admiration and affection, and gave him such prominence throughout his too brief yet brilliant career. By his comprehensiveness of intellect, his accurate and solid judgment, his kind, generous and noble heart, his almost miraculous quickness of perception, and his rapid execution, Nature stamped him as a leader of men. His whole life illustrated and vindicated his title to that distinction. Called by the people at an early age to represent them in the House of Representatives of the United States, a place among the most distinguished, controlling his fellow-members, was immediately assigned to him. The discriminating judgment of his associates soon called him to the chair of the House, where he won new and unsurpassed honors for his ability and fidelity in the discharge of the duties of the office. He then filled with unexcelled ability and faithfulness the office of governor of Georgia, and was again returned to Congress to win new claims to public gratitude. He was next called to fill one of the highest positions in the Cabinet of President Buchanan. Equal to the performance of its high duties, "clear in his office," his zeal, fidelity and capacity placed his name high on the roll of his most distinguished predecessors.

In the proud effort of the late Confederate States to assert and vindicate their sovereignty and to maintain the rights and liberties of the people, he was conspicuous on the side of his country, in the council and in the field. As president of the convention he aided by his great talents and ripe experience to erect a new government, and he buckled on his sword to give permanence and security to the great work, still struggling in the cause of truth and right, still worshiping at the altar of patriotism. When the fortune of war wrested the sword from his own hand and from the hands of the brave and chivalrous champions of liberty, and blasted the hopes of his countrymen, he yielded to inevitable fate with a spirit unbroken and a heart undaunted, without a stain on his honor or a single unworthy concession to the power which overthrew the right.

Death found him at the zenith of his glorious career, standing at his post, a faithful sentinel ready for duty amidst the fiery deluge of rage, hate and corruption which was overwhelming and consuming the last hopes of liberty in his native land.

This is but a faint outline of the public career of the great man whose loss we deplore. Amid all these public cares, we all know his zeal, fidelity and constancy in the discharge of every duty connected with his office of trustee. Here he was never wearied in well-doing. His private life commends him no less to our love and affection than his public life to our gratitude and admiration. In all the relations of private life—as son, husband, father, relative, friend, citizen—his daily walk from youth to the grave was a model of excellency, of affection and fidelity, and sheds naught but joy, happiness and blessing upon family, friends and society.

Therefore the committee would recommend the adoption of the following resolutions:

Resolved, That it is the sense of this body that in the death of Howell Cobb the State of Georgia has lost one of the most gifted and distinguished of her sons, the University one of its brightest ornaments, and this Board one of its ablest and most useful members.

Resolved, That this Board tenders to the afflicted family of our lamented associate the expression of its sincere condolence and sympathy in the great affliction which it has pleased God to visit them.

Resolved, That it is the desire of this Board, as representatives of the University, to obtain permission to inscribe upon the monument to be erected to the memory of Howell Cobb its estimate of his character and virtues, and that the proper steps be taken to secure the permission of his family to carry out this wish.

Resolved, That these resolutions be spread upon the records of this Board, and that a copy of them be communicated by the Secretary to the widow of our deceased brother.

R. Toombs, *Chairman*.

FRIENDSHIP'S OFFERINGS.

Oh, your desert speaks loud; and I should wrong it
To lock it in the wards of covert bosom,
When it deserves with characters of brass
A forted residence 'gainst the tooth of time,
And razure of oblivion.

Stand free and fast,
And judge him by no more than what you know
Ingenuously, and by the right-laid line
Of truth, he truly will all styles deserve,
Of wise, good, just; a man, both soul and nerve.

V.

FRIENDSHIP'S OFFERINGS.

OFFERING OF WM. HOPE HULL, ESQ.

AUGUSTA, November 4, 1868.

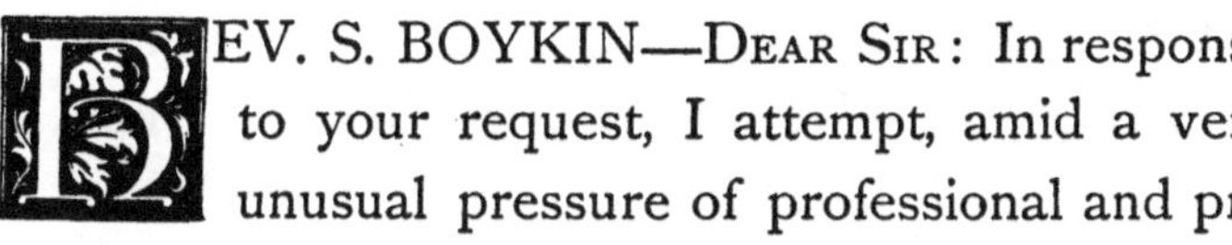EV. S. BOYKIN—DEAR SIR: In response to your request, I attempt, amid a very unusual pressure of professional and private business, to write a brief memorial of a departed friend.

I feel deeply my inadequacy to the task. My attachment for him, and my grief for his loss, still fresh and poignant, cannot be put in words; and when the memories of the past crowd upon me, I can only sit in sad reverie, and think of the associations sundered for ever, and of delightful intercourse unbroken for years, but never to be had again. I can only think of him and speak of him in terms of unqualified eulogy; for his faults, whatever they may have been, were never apparent to me, and *now* I could not be persuaded of their existence. I do not pretend to write as an impartial critic, but as a warm, devoted friend.

My acquaintance with Gov. Cobb commenced in my childhood, but my intimate association with him dates from the spring of 1840, when I was admitted to the Bar of the Western Circuit, at which he had practiced about four years previously.

A more genial and delightful society has seldom been collected than was the Bar of the Western Circuit twenty-eight years ago. They were not perhaps very learned in the books; they were not as assiduous in business as lawyers are now; but in native talent, in shrewd knowledge of mankind, and above all in the qualities of social good-fellowship, in kindly humor and a disposition to pass life agreeably, they were not easily surpassed. It is sufficient to those who remember them to recall the names of Judge Harris, Judge Dougherty, Gen. Harden, Mr. Paine, Col. Stanford, B. H. Overby, and A. J. Peeples, besides others whom I do not name because they still survive, to prove all that I have said of the character of their social intercourse.

In this brilliant circle our friend was pre-eminent. He was the life of every company, the universal favorite. He was in the freshness of his youth, overflowing with animal spirits, warm-hearted and generous, and of a good-humor that never failed. Everybody called him by the familiar name of "Howell;" his room in the hotels was the nightly resort of all who could spare the time for society. Political excitement was running high, and he was a warm partisan, but it made no difference in his social intercourse. Whigs sought his room as constantly as Democrats, and enjoyed his cordial good-humor as heartily. He was no *raconteur* of anecdotes, nor did he utter prepared witticisms that could be quoted. Everything was the spontaneous, natural utterance of the moment, and consisted in a steady, uniform flow of good-natured banter, that kept the whole company in the same pleasant temper with himself. He never said ill-natured things; he was never sarcastic, and no one was ever mortified or wounded by anything that he uttered.

Though these qualities were shaded somewhat in after years, when the cares of life pressed on him, yet they characterized him up to a late period of his life. I believe it may be said with literal truth that no one was ever tired of his company.

I have said that his unfailing good-humor lasted to a late period of his life. The date at which it left him was the date of the subjugation of his country. After that dreadful blow he never was (in this respect) the same man. He was as kind-hearted as ever, as loving and gentle; and he often, by an effort, would call back some of the old humor, but those who knew him well could see that it was forced. The buoyancy and elasticity of spirit was broken, and he was a sad and melancholy man. It would be strange if it had not been so, for he loved his native South with a warm and passionate devotion; and to see her crushed and bleeding under the heel of oppressión and have no power to help, and to look into her future and see the dark clouds in which it was shrouded crushed him down as no mere personal sorrows could have done.

But I will not dwell longer on this theme.

As a lawyer, Gov. Cobb was as successful as could be expected under the circumstances in which he practiced. His influence with juries was always great, and his strong, clear sense seized at once on the controlling points of a case, and he unraveled intricate facts with consummate skill. He would easily have taken the lead in his profession if his energies had been devoted to it. But he was only twenty-seven years of age when he was elected to Congress, and from that time to the close of the war his attention was given to public affairs.

Since our subjugation he devoted himself anew to the law, and showed how easily he could master it when he made the proper efforts.

Of his political career I have no occasion to speak. Everybody knows it, and it will of course be judged of by the different standards of men's diverging opinions.

Those who knew him best, however, will unite in bearing testimony to his ardent love for his country and the sincerity with which he sought her welfare. Whatever mistakes he may have made as to the *means*, the *ends* he sought were the happiness and prosperity of his country.

But it is neither as a lawyer nor as a politician, nor in any public capacity, that I love to contemplate his character. I think of him as the man, as the friend, as the companion; and I feel what is lost to the little world that was around *him*, rather than to the great world in which he was one of the actors. A more noble, princely heart never beat; a more gentle and loving spirit never passed away. He might have done *wrong* things—he could by no possibility have done a *mean* thing. His charity was unbounded, his love universal. He never, as I believe, knowingly and unnecessarily inflicted pain on any living thing. He never failed to do a kindness if it came in his way. Sometimes he denounced what he considered baseness in terms so strong that one who did not know him might have called it hate to the individual; but it was not so. He had no hatred in his composition; and no one would ever have asked in vain for his help if placed where it was needed. His generosity in giving to the needy was profuse.

Perhaps he could claim the less credit for this in that he never valued money, and did not bestow a regret on parting with it; but in this matter he did more. He gave in secret; he let not his right hand know what his left did. I have heard many a time, through accidental channels, of acts of large liberality that I had never heard alluded to by him, and do not doubt that there were many of which I never heard. It was this universal good-will that made him so universal a favorite.

No man had more devoted friends, because none felt more warmly the sentiment of friendship himself. While he was kind and generous to all, for his friends he had an affection that had no bounds.

He was the most unselfish person I ever knew; and when we reflect that he was ambitious, and that ambition is the most selfish of passions, we can appreciate the nobleness of soul that was always looking to the happiness of others and working for their success.

I will not prolong this letter. The universal sorrow so sincerely manifested for his loss shows that those who knew him need no one to tell them what he was. I will only add a single circumstance.

When I returned from Athens after his burial, I was sitting in the second-class car on the railroad, and heard the conversation of three colored men sitting near me. I soon discovered that they had been Gen. Cobb's slaves in former times, and that they had gone from South-west Georgia to Athens to attend his funeral.

I entered into some conversation with them about him. The most intelligent of them said to me:

"Sir, all that the preachers said of him was true, and very well as far as it went; but they did not say enough. If you want to know what a noble man he was, ask those who were his servants. They know it better than any one else."

He was indeed a nobleman of God's own making; a princely soul, a type of the Southern gentleman, such as we shall not easily find again.

Respectfully,

WM. HOPE HULL.

FROM REV. J. L. M. CURRY, D. D.

RICHMOND, VA., December 24, 1868.

I first knew Howell Cobb when I was a mere boy, fourteen years of age, at the University of Georgia. Then he was a promising young lawyer and an ardent Democrat. The party excitement "ran high," and Clarke county was opposed in politics to the young politician; but I remember distinctly, in the discussions that took place between the friends of the opposing parties, the courteous respect and warm attachment manifested for him by Judge Charles Dougherty, then the leader of the Whig party in Georgia, and the unusual popularity of Mr. Cobb with the "common people." Incapable of judging of the merits of the disputants, a speech of Mr. Cobb's made a deep impression, however, on my youthful mind by its clearness, fervor, directness and eloquence. Mr. Cobb was kind to me then, when I was a boy; spoke words of encouragement and hope and friendly regard; and when I subsequently met him in public life, it was easy for my early admiration to ripen into mature friendship.

I entered the United States Congress with Mr. Buchanan's administration, remaining a member until the first of January, 1860, when I retired to do what I could to secure the secession of Alabama. During that period, Mr. Cobb was Secretary of the Treasury. A former acquaintance, relationship to his wife, nativity in the same State, coincidence of political opinion, common sympathies in the imminent sectional struggle, threw me into intimate intercourse with him, which continued without interruption until his death. During much of the time that I was in Washington, scarce a week passed that I did not meet him in the unreserve of his own family, and I therefore had opportunities that few possessed for knowing the inner man in a superior degree. It is well known that Mr. Buchanan's administration encountered the bitterest opposition from the Republican party and that fragment of the Democratic party which supported Judge Douglas in his peculiar views. Charges of corruption, extravagance and malfeasance in office were unsparingly made against high officials. The Kansas troubles, John Brown's raid, the long contest for the Speakership and its exciting incidents, the Charleston Convention, the rupture in the Democratic party, and the Presidential election were inflammable causes, that aggravated political strife and alienated personal friendships. The angry and embittered contests were fretting asunder the bands of cohesion that had hitherto united the separate States in political compact. During these troublous times, Gov. Cobb was a general favorite; his "receptions" were crowded, and extreme Republicans often spoke to me of his unfailing good-humor, his contagious cheerfulness, his frankness, his patriotism, his devotion to duty and his official purity and incorruptibleness. No whisper affecting his honor was breathed. No stain of slander blurred the mirror of his public reputation.

In the administration of his office, distribution of patronage, interpretation of revenue laws, Gov. Cobb was scrupulously careful and conscientious. I was often impressed by his transparency of character, his fearless fidelity to right and duty, his unselfishness, his reliance upon principle, his rigid adherence to constitutional obligations, and his unfaltering confidence in the honesty and good sense of the masses.

Gov. Cobb had as few of the arts of the mere politician, the tricks of the craft, as any one I ever met in the public councils. He had no disguises nor concealments. He was a bold statesman, frank and true, and honest and courageous. When he despaired of State equality and constitutional justice for the minority section, he threw himself into the preparatory struggle with all the ardor of his noble nature, and counted all personal sacrifices as mere dross in comparison with the honor and welfare of his beloved South.

When the deputies from the sovereign States of South Carolina, Georgia, Alabama, Florida, Mississippi and Louisiana met in Montgomery to form a Provisional General Government for those States, Gov. Cobb was unanimously chosen as the President of the Congress. His large experience as a member and Speaker of the House of Representatives of the United States Congress admirably fitted him for that position, and he discharged its delicate duties to the entire satisfaction of the body. Few political convocations have ever met with graver responsibilities or a more scrupulous sense of the solemn obligations devolved on them by a confiding constituency. In addition to the general legislation necessary to organize a new government in all its departments, to provide an adequate financial system, to raise, equip and support an army, to put in operation all the machinery for a political experiment suddenly subjected to severest pressure, the Congress was compelled to frame a Provisional Constitution for the nascent Confederate States. It was thought proper also to adopt a Constitution for the permanent government of the Confederacy. In all this action, whether in framing statute or organic laws, Gov. Cobb took a prominent and influential part. The discipline, training and experience of the Bar and Congressional life gave him an eminent fitness for this work. His thorough acquaintance with the minute details of the *practical* operations of the Federal Government made his services invaluable. His speeches, not numerous, were short, cogent, lucid, vigorous, characterized by large grasp and wide scope and shrewd forecast. They were not the utterances of temporizing expediency, but the enunciation of principles, bold thoughts, running ahead of the present, and guarded like "the wise discourse which looks before and after."

Gov. Cobb, Mr. Stephens and Mr. Toombs, Georgia's three great statesmen, and others, sought to engraft in a modified form upon the Permanent Constitution a feature assimilating it somewhat to the British Constitution, in its idea of ministerial responsibility. Their speeches on that subject would have reflected credit on the British Parliament in the days of Fox and Pitt and Burke, or on the American Congress in the purer and better days of the republic, when the great Triumvirate were without peer or rival. Instead of yielding to the sagacious suggestions of these philosophical statesmen, the Congress ventured only upon this amendment of the former system of dependence and irresponsibility; "Congress may by law grant to the principal officer in each of the Executive Departments a seat upon the floor of either House, with the privilege of discussing any measures appertaining to his department."

The permanent Constitution, as ratified, is a conclusive refutation of all the malicious charges against the Confederate States of a purpose to establish a monarchy or overthrow constitutional liberty. The New York *Herald* republished the Constitution with an editorial commendation of its judicious improvements and changes, and suggested its acceptance by the North as a proper settlement of all existing difficulties.

Taken as a whole, the Provisional Congress was an assembly of men of very superior ability. Such deputies as Withers, Chestnut, Rhett, Memminger and Barnwell, of South Carolina; Stephens, Toombs, Hill, Bartow, Nisbet and T. R. R. Cobb, of Georgia; Walker, Smith, Shorter and Chilton, of Alabama; Harris, Harrison, Brooke and Clayton, of Mississippi; Kenner, Sparrow and Conrad, of Louisiana; and, later, Wigfall and Hemphill, of Texas; and Hunter and Rives and President Tyler, of Virginia, were illustrations of the advanced civilization of the South, and the popular appreciation of the kind of men who were needed in that formative and perilous period. It will not be questioned that when the Provisional Government ceased its functions, Gov. Cobb had established a reputation as a wise, able and sagacious statesman, inferior to none of his associates, while he certainly had a stronger hold than any upon the affections of his fellow-members.

Criticisms upon Congressional legislation during the war have been, since the surrender, severe and numerous. The difficulties of the situation were irremediable by statutes. Perils would not "down" at legislative bidding; nor would armies and coin come forth from hiding-places upon a Congressional call. No organic laws, no prevision of statesmanship, no financial skill, no legislation however perfect, could increase population or make one man equal to six, or multiply indefinitely the productive capacities of rude manufactories, or keep a necessarily-inflated currency at par with gold in a constantly-narrowing field of circulation. The struggle betwixt the Confederate States and the United States was not a struggle betwixt adverse legislatures, but a terrible contest of arms; and all the skill and patriotism and courage and intelligence and devotion of our chivalrous and noble people could not perpetually resist preponderating *avoirdupois* and limitless physical resources. No legislation could provide for all the exigencies of adverse battle. "War," says an ancient historian, "least of all things proceeds on definite principles, but adapts most of its contrivances from itself to suit the occasion." Gov. Cobb saw that not in the halls of Congress, but in the tented field (alas! how often untented and shelterless!), the issue was to be decided; and having advised secession, he felt impelled by a conscientious sense of duty to share all the dangers which were forced upon a people desiring only peace and freedom.

Gov. Cobb was not what is called a hard student. He was too social in his temperament, too fond of "goodlie companie," for severe application and midnight oil; and yet, when novel and great questions were presented, he thought closely and intensely. Duty and conscience guided him inflexibly in his opinions and actions.

I most admired Gov. Cobb as a man in his social relations, where he exhibited the docility of a child, the tenderness of a woman, the ardor of friendship, sympathy for youth, warm-hearted Southern hospitality, and where domestic virtues shone forth in their pure attractiveness. In his public life he bears the closest scrutiny, but those who got nearest to him and entered the *penetralia* of his big heart, knew best how to love him, when living, and now, to mourn for him when dead.

Yours truly,

J. L. M. Curry.

From the Hon. Hiram Warner, Judge of the Supreme Court of Georgia.

The sudden death of Gen. Cobb is an *irreparable* loss to the people of his native State. No living man had a stronger hold upon their confidence and affection than he whose loss they now so sincerely deplore. Gifted by nature with a strong, vigorous intellect, cultivated and improved by laborious study, and an active experience with his fellow-men both socially and politically, he was a man of *mark* amongst the brightest intellects and most eminent statesmen of our country. Who can estimate the loss of such a man in the present disturbed condition of the political affairs of the State? Possessing a sound, discriminating judgment, with enlarged, comprehensive views, stimulated by an ardent patriotism for the permanent welfare of the whole country upon the basis of constitutional liberty, he was, especially at the present time, a safe, discreet, conservative counselor to the people of Georgia, to whose interest and permanent welfare he was ever intensely devoted. Who shall supply his place?

The question is much more easily *asked* than *answered.*

As a statesman he had acquired a national reputation of which the most unscrupulous and vindictive political partisan cannot deprive him. His past political record will vindicate his sterling worth and eminent ability, whenever the sober judgment of the American people shall perform its appropriate functions. As a lawyer he occupied the front rank at the Bar of his native State. With a fine person, a clear, discriminating mind, of quick perception, united with a strong, vigorous, comprehensive power of thought, he had the capacity to analyze the most complicated legal question and present it to the Court in its simple elements. Those who have witnessed his arguments before the Supreme Court of the State cannot fail to have discovered with what wonderful facility he dissected and presented to the Court the main controlling points in the record of a cause, so that the simplest mind could readily understand and comprehend them. It requires the highest order of a well-disciplined intellect to accomplish this result, for which Gen. Cobb was so eminently distinguished. His great argument before the Supreme Court of Milledgeville upon the unconstitutionality of the Stay Law will long be remembered by those who heard it. The counsel who argued the case in favor of the constitutionality of the law had elaborately discussed the distinction between the *right* of a party under his contract, and the *remedy* to enforce that right, endeavoring to maintain that the Legislature had entire power and control over the *remedy* to enforce the obligation of contracts. Their reasoning was metaphysical, ingenious and plausible, well calculated to obscure and render *nugatory* the great constitutional principle involved in the issue. When Gen. Cobb rose to reply, who that was present can ever forget his manly form as he then stood before the Court, his countenance beaming with intelligence, seemingly deeply impressed with the importance of the question, as well as the fundamental principles of the law which then devolved upon him to vindicate and maintain? After a brief statement of the facts of the case, he soon came down to his work, and *right well did he perform it.* The subtle, plausible arguments of his adversaries were fairly examined—their fallacy exposed with a mental power and legal logic rarely equaled and never surpassed.

"What," said he, "upon *principle*, is a legal *right* worth without a legal *remedy* to enforce that legal right? What is a right under a contract *worth*, when one of the parties to it may be deprived of *the remedy* to enforce it which the law gave him at the time the contract was made?" He then proceeded to show that the Constitution prohibited the Legislature from passing any law *impairing* the obligation of contracts, and showed most conclusively, from the decisions of the Supreme Court of the United States, that the law in question *did impair* the obligation of contracts, and eloquently demanded that the *integrity* of the Federal Constitution should be maintained as expounded by the Supreme Court of the United States. This matchless argument, to be fully appreciated, must have been heard; its *truthfulness*, its mental power, its unanswerable logic, the manly vigor with which it was delivered, cannot be exhibited on paper;

all that we can do is to simply remark that it was one of the best forensic efforts of the gigantic intellect of Howell Cobb when in the full vigor and strength of his professional manhood.

Again we repeat in these times of demoralization and political degeneracy, Who can supply his place? What shall we say of his social qualities in our past intercourse with him as a companion and friend? The very soul of honor and generous magnanimity, his *equal* in kindness of heart, generous hospitality, and all that is calculated to endear man to his fellow-man, is rarely to be found in any country. It is painful to contemplate the fact that we shall never again be permitted to behold his cheerful countenance in this world, or to meet him in those social gatherings to which his presence always contributed so much to instruct, entertain and enliven. But he has been stricken down in the pride and vigor of his manhood by Him who does all things for the best, and we must submit to the stern decree of an all-wise Providence; yet we can cherish in our hearts a fond and kind remembrance of our departed friend, and endeavor to imitate his manly virtues; for, take him all in all, we shall seldom look upon his like again.

Gen. Cobb as a Statesman and Lawyer.

Milledgeville, July 21, 1869.

Mr. Boykin: Ordinary men should pass to the tomb unattended but by the regrets and remembrances of the narrow circle in which they had moved and in which only their existence had been felt; yet it so happens that, instead of quietly inurning mediocrities, indiscreet friendship, too often aided by the press, seeks to prolong reputations ephemeral in their nature beyond the limits which Truth and Justice allot, and in thus attempting to embalm them has exhausted the beautiful amber of language which should have been reserved for the good and great who stamp their image on the age and constitute its renown.

I have on this occasion, from the cause assigned, most sensibly felt my extreme poverty of felicitous diction—such as should have been employed in the delineation of a man like the late Gen. Howell Cobb; and to that consciousness I beg you to ascribe my long delay in complying with your request of furnishing for publication in the memorial you are getting up, my estimate of him as a statesman and lawyer.

I proceed to give it without any effort at rhetorical embellishment.

For the last ten years of his public life I regarded him as belonging to the highest class of statesmen—those who shape the measures and guide the fortunes of nations—those who act on public sentiment and who are in turn reacted on by the forces which they have put in motion or accelerated; of that class who are too wise to attempt to control events or to force the passions and prejudices and interests of a people to conform to what are called political principles; of that class who make their political opinions subservient to the march of the age, and, as new facts arise or a new exigency presents itself, modify those opinions so as to meet an altered condition.

This habit of mind necessarily generates a large and generous toleration of differences of opinion and action alike with friends and adversaries.

Such toleration is the infallible mark of a noble and great mind and of the highest statesmanship. A better specimen of this class than Gen. Cobb I have not known.

I have rarely, in a pretty long life in which I

have casually been brought into intercourse with some of the most distinguished statesmen of the country, met with any one who, upon approach, continued to impress me so favorably as did Gen. Cobb.

Whilst it is generally true of celebrated men, as of landscapes, that "distance lends enchantment to the view," and that the admiration felt proves an illusion when the object is near, yet it was not so with this remarkable man, whose simplicity and frankness of character, joyous disposition, delightful manners, all informed and regulated by common sense, inspired one with love, and at the same time increased our admiration as we surveyed with greater accuracy the proportions of his physical and mental organization. They appeared to be in perfect equilibrium. Massive in frame, the mind was solid and strong. It owed nothing of its manifestations to ornament.

The "tout ensemble" is best typified by one of those Grecian temples of the Doric order erected to Jupiter, designed to be eternal, and which, after the lapse of more than twenty centuries, though defaced by the barbarian and by the hand of time, in its remains continues to exhibit its wonderful beauty, the sense of which increases the more it is contemplated.

In a letter of this kind, good taste forbids that I should speak of the measures originated and supported by him whilst in Congress, as they belong to biography and to history. The same propriety forbids comment whilst he was at the head of the Treasury.

It is enough for fame that in the most advanced period of the growth and prosperity of the United States, when the States had spread from the Atlantic to the Pacific, and their population had increased from five to twenty-five millions, he was deemed worthy by the American people to be the successor of Alexander Hamilton, Dallas, Gallatin and our own illustrious William H. Crawford.

At the close of the war he returned to the practice of law. Withdrawn for so many years from the contests of the Bar, it was reasonable to expect that he could bring but little legal learning to the discharge of the duties which might be required of him as an advocate. Yet in this he surprised the whole profession. If, indeed, science is but organized knowledge, he soon made it apparent that he was thoroughly acquainted with the general principles on which the vast structure of municipal law has been erected; and, with facility he applied them, in the resolution of the questions he was called upon to discuss.

It was no doubt true that his familiarity with "cases" and "precedents" was very limited, compared with that of some of his contemporaries; but the very absence of their citation, and the want of reliance on the thoughts and reasoning of other men, gave freshness and vigor to his own mind, and constituted the charm of his masterly arguments.

His commanding power consisted in his reliance on his own faculties of analogy and illustration. Confining himself strictly to the facts of the record, and on no occasion arguing upon anything without it, he never wasted his strength or exhausted the patience of the Court in the discussion of trivial matters which could not constitute an element of the decision to be made. Nor did he repeat, but he unfolded his positions with an admirable method and with an accumulating force, in precise and perspicuous language, and with a tact that satisfied every one that he possessed the highest skill.

So complete were his arguments on all occasions that it was impossible for the dullest judge who ever wore a wig or gown not thoroughly to comprehend him.

It is by such advocacy as Gen. Cobb employed that a Bench can be much assisted in the analysis of the cases it is called on to determine.

Of the many causes argued before the Supreme Court in which he participated, I apprehend no one will be longer remembered by the Bench and Bar in attendance than the discussion in June, 1866, upon *the unconstitutionality of Stay Laws in general.*

Arrayed in opposition to him were some of the most distinguished lawyers of Georgia, viz.: Ex-Governor, now Chief Justice Brown, Judge Linton Stephens, Barnard Hill, Esq., Samuel Hall, Esq., and in the closing debate the Honorable Alexander H. Stephens, assisted, in the protracted discussion which ensued, by Judge Lyon. Gen. Cobb maintained himself against this imposing force with signal ability and address. It has never been my lot to witness so much mind in ardent conflict in the discussion of a great constitutional question.

It may be justly said, without disparagement to his distinguished opponents, that he came out of this great intellectual tournament unscarred by the blows of his antagonists and with augmented reputation.

In fine, at the Bar of the Supreme Court of Georgia, which includes very many of the best intellects of the State, he stood prominently forward in its front rank; and whilst it would be invidious to assign to him the pre-eminence which ardent friendship claims for him, now that he has passed from the stage of action, of having been *primus inter pares*, I will say, what the public voice will respond to, that as a great advocate he had *no* superior.

His sudden death, in the very prime of his faculties, and at a moment when his native State most needed his wise and practical counsel to guide her in finding the best path to returning quiet and prosperity, was *an irreparable loss*.

Death has transferred him as "a bright particular star" to that constellation which adorns our political firmament. His name is now grouped in it with Jackson, Baldwin, Early, Crawford, Trou, Forsyth and Berrien, whose united fame has made, and will for ever perpetuate, the glory of Georgia.

Very respectfully,

IVERSON LOUIS HARRIS.

www.ingramcontent.com/pod-product-compliance
Lightning Source LLC
LaVergne TN
LVHW010225110826
845151LV00004B/1187
9781425526146